Peter Gisson

VINCENT
NOVELLO
–AND
COMPANY

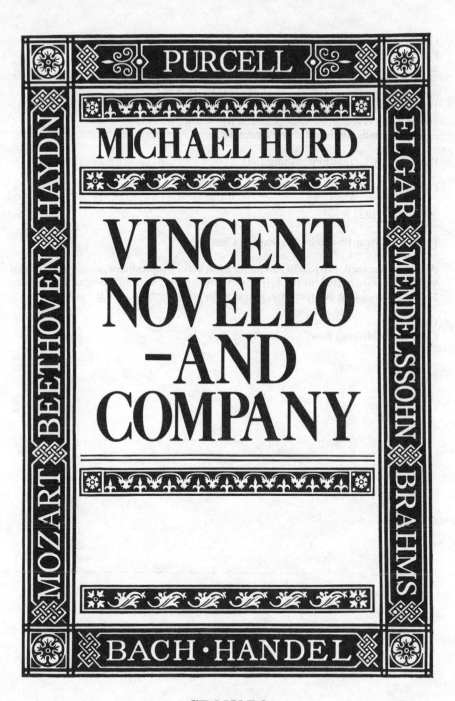

PURCELL

HAYDN   ELGAR

MICHAEL HURD

BEETHOVEN   MENDELSSOHN

VINCENT
NOVELLO
– AND
COMPANY

MOZART   BRAHMS

BACH · HANDEL

GRANADA
London Toronto Sydney New York

Granada Publishing Limited
Frogmore, St Albans, Herts AL2 2NF
and
36 Golden Square, London W1R 4AH
866 United Nations Plaza, New York, NY 10017, USA
117 York Street, Sydney, NSW 2000, Australia
100 Skyway Avenue, Rexdale, Ontario M9W 3A6, Canada
61 Beach Road, Auckland, New Zealand

Published by Granada Publishing 1981

Copyright © Michael Hurd 1981

ISBN 0 246 11733 8

Printed in Great Britain by Mackays of Chatham

Granada ®
Granada Publishing ®

CONTENTS

CONTENTS

LIST OF ILLUSTRATIONS

ACKNOWLEDGEMENTS

Since that moment in 1962 when I signed my first contract in the awesome surroundings of their Wardour Street board room I have been fascinated by the publishing house of Novello & Company, Ltd. As a composer my relations with them have been singularly happy, and it is now my great pleasure to record the fact.

In the special circumstances that arose during the writing of this book, however, I must surely have tried their patience to the limit. Yet from every member of the staff I have received nothing but kindness, help and encouragement. Some of them have been in a special position to advise and instruct me, and it will not, I trust, seem invidious if I name them. They are: the company secretary, Bernard Axcell; the warehouse manager, Bert Daws; the printing works manager, Allan Darby; the foreman engraver, Leslie Ellis; and the acquisitions editor, Margaret Pace (Mrs H. S. P. Brooke). Five members of the firm now retired, Henry S. P. Brooke, Eldon Ffitch, Harry Fowle, John Littleton and Henry Littleton, have also been particularly helpful. To all these people, and to every member of the Novello staff, I owe a great debt.

I am also most grateful to the librarian of the Brotherton collection at Leeds University, Mr D. Cox, and his staff (in particular Mr C. D. W. Sheppard, the sub-librarian) for their assistance in helping me to examine the Novello Cowden Clarke Collection. Quotations from the material contained in this archive appear by kind permission of the university authorities, and the donor, Contessa Bona Gigliucci.

Quotations from the Novello private library and files appear by kind permission of Novello & Co. Ltd. Quotations from letters and documents at present in private hands appear by kind permission of the individual owners. The keeper of portraits at the Royal College of Music has kindly given permission to quote the George Grove–Edith Oldham letter of 4 March 1894 which first appeared in print in *George Grove, 1820–1900* by Percy M. Young (Macmillan, 1980). The letter of 28 January 1839 from Vincent Novello to his wife, which appears by kind permission of the Leeds University authorities, was first published in *The Cowden Clarkes* by Richard Altick (OUP, 1948).

Michael Hurd
West Liss, Hampshire, April 1981

CHAPTER ONE

VINCENT NOVELLO

Vincent Novello became a publisher more by accident than design. For when, in May 1811, he first appeared in print with two folio volumes of sacred music 'as performed at the Royal Portuguese Chapel in London',[1] he can scarcely have guessed where his action would lead. He was not by nature a business man–rather, a practical working musician with an intense, but somewhat capricious, enthusiasm for musical scholarship. Moreover he was too busy earning a living to have time to plot the intricacies of a wholehearted publishing venture. What he had on offer in 1811 was a collection of music that seemed to him to fulfil a need, and which might perhaps ensure him a place among the composers he so greatly admired. His was largely a benevolent act–a wish to share the things he believed in and which experience had taught him were good and useful. There was nothing to suggest that he had planted a seed that was to have a profound effect not only upon his own life and the lives of his family, but also upon the future development of music in Great Britain.

He was born in London on 6 September 1781 at 240 Oxford Road (later Street), where his father, Giuseppe Novello, pursued the trade of pastrycook. Giuseppe came from Tonengo, a small town in Piedmont, which in those days formed part of the Kingdom of Sardinia. Born in 1744, he emigrated to England in 1771 and began to earn a living by selling cakes in the London streets. Evidently he prospered, for in March 1776 he was able to purchase a leasehold on '240 Oxford Road, opposite Park Lane, for 14 years for £55'.[2] By that time he had also been four years married to a Norfolk girl, Joan Wins, and had started a family. Little is known of his early struggles, but two pocket-books have survived to give testimony to the hazards of eighteenth-century childbirth. One after another, beginning on 30 March 1775 and continuing in almost annual succession, the arrival of sons and daughters is recorded 'natto morto'.[3] On such pages the rough, uneducated handwriting is pale and ghostly, as if he could scarcely bring himself to frame the pitiful news. At one point the words appear blotched with tears. But at last there are pages where the ink thickens and the handwriting is bold and triumphant, and on these are set down the birth dates of two sons, Francesco and Vincenzo, 29 March 1779 and 6 September 1781.

Whether music played any part in the Novello ancestry is not known. Giuseppe's own parents, Francesco and Theresa, were of very humble origin and with them the line fades into obscurity. But doubtless they were like most Italian peasants and enjoyed the natural musicality that waits only upon favourable circumstance to blossom into genuine talent. With Giuseppe's two sons that moment arrived. Both became professional musicians–Francis (their names were anglicized very early on) as a capable bass singer, and Vincent as an outstanding organist, choir master, musical scholar, and prolific minor composer.

The sons of pastrycooks, however, could not at this period expect an elaborate education, and so far as music is concerned both appear to have been largely self-taught. According to his daughter, Mary Cowden Clarke, Vincent 'would slip away from meals, to use his recreation-time in "finding out chords" on an old pianoforte, when once he had "learnt his notes." These were taught him by a friend of his father, one Signor Quellici; and this was the only direct instruction [he] ever received'.[4]

Sometime in the early 1790s the two boys were sent to a school at Huitmille, near Boulogne, in order to add French to the Italian and English they already spoke. They returned in 1793 'by the last boat that left France before war was declared'.[5] Eager to seize every opportunity to extend his musical knowledge, Vincent now became a chorister at the Sardinian Embassy Chapel in Lincoln's Inn Fields. Here he came into contact with the elder Samuel Webbe, who was organist at the chapel, and with John Danby, organist of the Spanish Embassy Chapel in Manchester Square. Soon, it seems, he was able to act as their occasional deputy. By 1797, when he was scarcely sixteen years old, he had himself acquired an organist post–at the Portuguese Embassy Chapel in South Street, Grosvenor Square.

He remained here for twenty-five years. According to his daughter he was an excellent organist:

> When accompanying voices, he seemed to know, by intuition, which singer required aid; and he would, as it were, imperceptibly prompt, as well as support, the particular vocalist needing guidance. His sensitive ear followed the inner parts no less accurately than the more salient bass or soprano; and many an uncertain tenor, or wavering alto, would he–with his distinctive finger pressing slightly out their particular required note or passage–steady back to their appointed course . . . Not only was his own performance on the organ fine and potential, but his ability in conducting the vocal choir was supreme. It became a fashion to hear the service at the Portuguese Chapel; and South Street, on a Sunday, was thronged with carriages waiting outside, while their owners crowded to suffocation the small, taper-lighted space within.[6]

Under such circumstances Bach was explored, and the masses of Haydn and Mozart were heard for the first time in England. Vincent Novello rose to a position of considerable eminence in the London musical world. Indeed, his music-making had the happy effect of by-passing sectarian differences. Although the Portuguese Embassy Chapel was one of the seven places of worship reserved for Catholics in London in the days before the Emancipation Act of 1829 (there were four Embassy chapels in all), Protestants were equally drawn to the performances. It is typical of Vincent Novello that it should be the music that mattered, and artistic excellence.

He appears to have been most at his ease when in sole command of musical affairs. Significantly, he turned down a pressing offer from King George IV to become organist of the Chapel Royal in the Pavilion, Brighton. And a brief spell directing the orchestra (from the keyboard) when the fabulous Angelica Catalani's Italian opera company appeared at the Pantheon in 1812 seems to have been more than enough to satisfy any curiosity he may have felt for this notoriously temperamental field of musical activity. The organ loft was another matter. Twenty-five years at the Portuguese Embassy Chapel, a short spell in and around 1805 as organist of St Patrick's Chapel, Soho

Square, and three years (1840–43) at the Roman Catholic Chapel at Moorfields testify to his competence and enthusiasm. He seems also to have been a natural teacher. Twice a week for twenty-seven years he was content to appear as music master to the girls of Miss Campbell's school in Brunswick Square. For a while he also taught at a school in Clapton.

In grander spheres he was equally active. His name appears (1813) in the list of founder members of the Philharmonic Society–one of thirty 'Professors of Music' who constituted the cream of London's music-making. He directed many of the society's concerts at the old and new Argyll Rooms in Oxford Street, and in the spring of 1839 he 'presided at the organ' when the Choral Harmonists gave the first public performance in Great Britain of Beethoven's *Missa Solemnis*.[7] He was similarly engaged at the organ during the 1834 Westminster Abbey Festival; and, as a member of the Royal Society of Musicians, played viola in the orchestra it provided for the annual Festival of the Sons of the Clergy at St Paul's Cathedral.

Complementary to his work as a practical musician were his activities as a musical scholar. In this he was moved by a boundless enthusiasm not simply for the music of the Catholic Church, but for music of every denomination and type. He was to be seen in the opera house almost as regularly as in the organ loft. And if the operas of Mozart pleased him more than those of Rossini, he was merely expressing the preference of someone who had gone to the trouble of exploring both. The deeper his researches went, the more he was delighted with his discoveries. Some of his favourites, such as Thomas Attwood, Samuel Wesley and Mendelssohn, were his contemporaries and personal friends. Some–most importantly Purcell and Mozart–were to become, as it were, friends by proxy, so great was the enthusiasm he felt for their music.

In this aspect of his life he was helped and encouraged by the Revd Christian Latrobe (1757–1836). Latrobe had taken orders in the Church of the United (Moravian) Brethren in England, and was, besides being a competent composer (praised even by Haydn), a musicologist of significance. He welcomed the young Vincent Novello to the free run of his library, and was clearly of fundamental importance in the development of his musical curiosity and taste.

As a man, Vincent Novello might have stood as a model for Samuel Pickwick. He was, his daughter tells us:

about middle height; his person somewhat stout; his carriage and walk wonderfully energetic and purposeful; his hands and feet remarkably small and white. On a certain occasion, the shapeliness and delicacy of these latter were made obvious; when, going down to the shore to meet her father returning from a morning plunge in the sea, one of his daughters saw him take off his shoe and shake out the sand that had drifted in, leaving his fair stockingless foot revealed to view. No one seeing his boots or shoes would have guessed the small size of his foot; for he wore them of a magnitude more suited to a slipper-bath than to human dimension. He said he liked to have them *easy*; and the consequence was that they might have accommodated any amount of sea-sand in addition to the foot they shod, giving ready admission to whatever quantity chose to lodge there. His clothes were of an equally (what he called) *commodious* make; and his cravat was always tied loosely enough to allow for his chin reposing roomily therein, as well as his throat. He was early bald; losing the chief portion of his hair when he was no older than six-and-twenty. It preserved its brown colour for many years; and only latterly turned grey.

His manners, when in good health, were social, gay, and lively. Fond of conversation, he talked well and freely, when with those he intimately knew; but he was retiring—nay, shy—with strangers. He had a good deal of English reserve in his bearing towards those he met for the first time; though it wore off on acquaintance, and vanished altogether when he took a liking to them. He had a certain quiet pride, common to very modest men; conscious of innate merit, yet averse from self-assertion. With his chosen friends he was easy, genial, cordial. With them he gave way to mirth and good-fellowship; laughed, bantered, punned. He was a great punster...[8]

The 'quiet pride' described by his daughter amounted, in practice, to something more than she suspected. Although he was well aware that his abilities as a composer were infinitely less than those of the Purcells, Mozarts and Mendelssohns he idolized, Vincent Novello nevertheless considered himself to be what indeed he was—a man far above the ordinary. His will, dated 16 March 1844, ends typically in a provision that manages to combine natural philanthropy and common sense with an endearing touch of self-importance:

If it be considered that the interest of medical science can be promoted, or that any good can be done to the *living* by the anatomical examination of the *dead* remains, or by taking a cast of my skull etc, I request that this may be done in my case.[9]

Though in his general dealings with the world he was a mild, benevolent man, his passions could be roused at the thought of any injustice, especially where music was concerned. Writing to his young friend the composer and scholar Edward Rimbault (1816–76) on 24 July 1847, he indulges in a fine frenzy of righteous indignation:

As I am now collecting the materials for a *third* volume of Boyce's Services & Anthems, can you tell me where I can meet with any of his unpublished MSS?

I have applied to my friend Mr Goss under the impression that it was possible that some of Boyce's MSS might have been in the Cathedral to which he belonged: but it is evident that the "Parsons in power" at it (like the generality of clerical gangs who have got possession of the funds at the Cathedral Establishments, a considerable portion of which funds was intended for the support of Music & Musicians, but which these "dishonest Stewards" and cheating "money-changers in the Temple" have pocketed themselves, thereby impudently plundering & robbing the *useful* Members of their Church where such lazy drones, gormandizing gluttons, & locust-like vermin are employed)–I repeat that it is evident the "Proud, Priestly Pickpockets" of St Paul's Cathedral in the time of Dr Boyce neither valued his superior musical talents, nor encouraged his exertions in writing for their cathedral nor even *purchased a single Copy* of several of his finest productions, after he himself risked the expense of publishing them for the accommodation of Cathedral Choirs; for in the St Paul's Choir Books, so far from preserving any of the Pieces which he must have occasionally written *expressly* for the Church to which he belonged, & which consequently ought to have been peculiarly prized & preserved with particular care & veneration,– these books do not contain (according to the List with which Mr Goss has so courteously furnished me) even *half* of the *published* compositions by Boyce, that are to be commonly found in almost every respectable choir.

It is impossible for me to express the disgust, contempt, &

scorn I feel towards Parsons of this mean-souled, money-grasping, paltry, shabby, loathsome-spirited stamp: and I pride myself on being known as the *decided & open enemy* of such a despicable crew.

I disdain to conceal my opinion, as it is the result of long experience. I have been *behind the scenes*, as far as priestly acting is concerned; having (from my position as Organist) been thrown into familiar & continual intercourse with clerical pretenders of different kinds for nearly fifty years; and (with *very few* exceptions) I have, in the end, detected Parsons of every sect to be a set of self-interested, deceitful, mercenary, dictatorial, mischievously-meddling, sensual, bigoted, narrow-minded, mean-spirited, canting & hypocritical Imposters.

I remain, Dear Sir,
Your plain-spoken, straight
& frankly-sincere
Vincent Novello.[10]

In 1808 two important events changed the course of Vincent Novello's life. The first occurred on 7 February when his father died. His mother, about whom almost nothing is known, probably died some time before 1808, and when it came to dividing Giuseppe's small estate a dispute flared up briefly between the two brothers. This was eventually settled in Vincent's favour. The arbitrators held that because he had helped support his father, settled his debts and assumed responsibility for the lease on 240 Oxford Street, and had already given his brother £50, he was not obliged to make over any part of what little remained.

The second event had more far-reaching consequences. He met, and then on 17 August married, the young Mary Sabilla Hehl. Mary Hehl was the daughter of Simon Hehl and Elizabeth Field. She was born probably in 1789 or 1790 (her marriage certificate describes her in 1808 as a minor). It was rumoured that her father was the son of a German aristocrat whose name was not Hehl. He had been born in Frankfurt-am-Main in 1740, and had come to England in the early 1770s as the travelling companion of a tight-fisted Scottish baronet whom he had met in Italy. In London he took lodgings with a Mrs Field—an Irish woman, the widow of a British army officer—and promptly fell in love with her beautiful daughter. They married on 8 February 1780.

Simon and Elizabeth Hehl had three children: Mary Sabilla;

Catherine, who married a Mr John Collins; and Simon, who became a Captain of Foot Guards, and later Assistant Quartermaster General of Horse Guards, and whose own daughter (Mary Anne Hehl) became the celebrated Victorian actress Mrs Stirling.

The relationship between Vincent Novello and Mary Sabilla Hehl began, as it was to continue throughout their married life, in great tenderness. Vincent, as a letter written in 1839 proves, never forgot the details:

You must know, Dearest Mary, that there are four spots in London which have become my favourite haunts, & the very neighbourhood of which has become enchanted ground in my imagination. These are, first, the spot in Oxford Street at the corner of James Street, where I first met you one Evening shortly after the death of my dear Father, & when I felt as if I had been left alone in the world. I perfectly well remember that I was returning slowly home to my solitary supper (which I was obliged to go out to purchase for myself) when I unexpectedly beheld you quite close to my side–the kind manner in which you spoke to me–the soft & delicious tone of your charming voice–the frank & cheering way in which you expressed your sympathy with my melancholy & lonely situation–all made the deepest impression upon my heart (where they have remained unforgotten ever since) & the conversation wh. passed between us as I walked home with you to yr own house, is still fresh in my memory. It is to that Evening I date my resolution to endeavour to gain so rich a prize as your love, and to prevail upon you to become the constant companion of my future life.

The second spot is near the enclosure in St James' Park, under the pine trees in approaching Spring Gardens, where I first ven- tured to declare what was passing in my heart, & where you so generously consented (without the least affectation of prudery, or the silly pretence to indecision or reluctance, in which so many girls indulge themselves on such occasions) to become my wife.

The third spot, is the House in Park St where you lived so many years–including the adjoining place in Park Lane, where I waited to receive you as my bride, from the hands of your Father, on the morning of our Wedding-Day. The last & dearest spot of all is the old house in Oxford Street, where you first gave yourself to my arms–& where you continued for so many years

to bless my home with your cheerful & animating presence—and
forming the principal charm & greatest joy of my existence. May
heaven reward you, Dearest Mary, for all the unwearied tenderness you have shewn towards me and all the benefits of every
kind you have so profusely bestowed upon me ever since I have
known you.[11]

Though not an exceptional beauty (if portraits are to be relied upon),
Mary Sabilla was an attractive woman of great charm and considerable
intellectual accomplishment. She wrote and published a number of
essays and stories, under such engaging titles as *Adventures of a Brocade
Petticoat*, *A Day in Stowe Gardens* and *A Legend of Schlangenbad*, and in
1840 a novel entitled *Margaret, or The Daughter's Trial*. Her name
occurs frequently in the letters of Leigh Hunt and Charles Lamb, who
clearly admired her—though Hunt, who gave her the affectionate but
revealing nickname 'Wilful Woman', could never resist teasing her:

> Mary Novello
> I know not your fellow
> For having your way
> Both by night and by day.[12]

But if she wore the trousers in the Novello household, her primary
concern seems to have been to ensure a comfortable and happy home.
In this she was singularly successful. Thanks to Vincent's eminent
position in the musical world and her own intellectual and domestic
talents, 240 Oxford Street became a favourite meeting place for poets,
musicians, writers and painters: a kind of minor Parnassus, bourgeois
and comfortable, dedicated to the arts and good-fellowship. The
radical Leigh Hunt, lately emancipated from the Surrey gaol for his
libel against the Prince Regent, was a constant and appreciative visitor.
So too were Charles and Mary Lamb, Charles Cowden Clarke and his
young pupil John Keats—though Keats was to find that 'a complete
set-to of Mozart and Punning' was more than he could take on a
regular basis.

An echo of their high spirits and good humour is to be found in a
letter which Charles Lamb wrote in May 1830. In it he pokes gentle
fun at Vincent's incurable reverence for memorials and relics of great
men:

Pray write immediately to say "The book has come safe." I am anxious not so much for the autographs, as for that bit of hair brush. I enclose a cinder, which belonged to *Shield* when he was poor and lit his own fires. Any memorial of a great Musical Genius, I know, is acceptable; and Shield has his merits, though Clementi, in my opinion, is far above him in the Sostenuto. Mr Westwood desires his compliments, and begs to present you with a nail that came out of Jomelli's coffin, who is buried at Naples...[13]

A similar banter informs the letter of instruction he sent with the words of a *Serenata for Two Voices* he pretended he had written especially for the marriage of Charles and Mary Cowden Clarke—though in fact he had borrowed the entire piece from a minor eighteenth-century poet, John Hughes, making only a few simple adjustments:

To so great a master as yourself I have no need to suggest that the peculiar tone of the composition requires sprightliness, occasionally checked by tenderness, as in the second air–
          She smiles,–she yields,–she loves.
Again, you need not be told that each fifth line of the two first recitatives requires a crescendo.
    And your exquisite taste will prevent your falling into the error of Purcell, who at a passage similar to that in my first air,
          Drops his bow, and stands to hear,
directed the first violin thus:
          "Here the first violin must drop his *bow*."
    But besides the absurdity of thus disarming his principal performer of so necessary an adjunct to his instrument, in such an emphatic part of the composition too, which must have had a droll effect at the time, all such minutiae of adaptation are at this time of day very properly exploded, and Jackson of Exeter very fairly ranks them under the head of puns.
    Should you succeed in the setting of it, we propose having it performed (we have one very tolerable second voice here, and Mr Holmes, I dare say, would supply minor parts) at the Greyhound. But it must be a secret to the young couple till we can get the band in readiness.
          Believe me, dear Novello, yours truly,
            C. Lamb[14]

In her autobiography, that same daughter, Mary Cowden Clarke, paints in the background of Vincent Novello's social life:

> The evening parties...were marked by a judicious economy blended with the utmost refinement and good taste; the supper refection was of the simplest—Elia's "Chapter on Ears" eloquently recording the "friendly supper-tray" and the draught of "true Lutheran Beer" which succeeded to the feasts of music provided by the host's playing on the small but fine-toned chamber organ, which occupied one end of the graceful drawing-room. This was papered with a delicately-tinted pink colour, showing to advantage the choice water-colour paintings by Varley, Copley Fielding, Havell and Cristall that hung around. These artists were all personally known to Vincent Novello, and were not unfrequent visitors on these occasions. The floor was covered by a plain grey drugget, bordered by a beautiful garland of grapes and vine-leaves, designed and worked by my mother herself.[15]

The Novello circle was indeed remarkable for its catholicity—large enough to embrace the atheist Shelley and the Hambledon cricketer John Nyren, the tempestuous Maria Malibran and the eccentric Domenico Dragonetti (genius of the double bass). The composer of *Elijah* was as welcome as the author of *Frankenstein*, and the irascible Sam Wesley as honoured as both. The Novellos, in short, had a genius for friendship.

It was into this liberal, open-minded atmosphere that Vincent Novello's eleven children were born. Four died in infancy and childhood, and one at twenty-three, but the remaining six lived to old age. Of the seven who grew to maturity, four were outstandingly gifted.

CHAPTER TWO

THE NOVELLO FAMILY

Vincent and Mary wasted little time in starting a family. The first child, Mary Victoria, was born on 22 June 1809, some ten months after their wedding. Others followed almost annually until the arrival of Charles Vincent in 1823. Of the eleven, four did not live long enough to reveal any special talent. Sydney Vincent, born in 1816, died in 1820; Julia Harriet, born in 1820, lived little more than a year; and Florence, born in 1822, died before her tenth birthday. Charles Vincent, the last of the brood, died in the year of his birth.

Mary Victoria lived from 1809 to 1898. She inherited her mother's literary gifts and her father's capacity for hard work. In consequence she became not only the family's chief chronicler, but also a writer of world-wide reputation. On 5 July 1828 she married a man many years older than herself, Charles Cowden Clarke.

Born in 1787, Charles Cowden Clarke was not much younger than Vincent Novello. In his early twenties he had been a teacher in his father's school at Enfield. There he had met and profoundly influenced towards poetry the young John Keats. In due course he became intimately involved in Leigh Hunt's circle and a constant visitor at the Novello household. By 1822 he had become resident in the hospitable home: not merely a lodger, but part of the family and much loved by all the children.

Despite the difference in their ages, or maybe because of it, the Cowden Clarke marriage was a resounding success. Each was the other's closest confidante and warmest admirer. Each encouraged the other in their indefatigable literary pursuits, both favouring the ornate and rather involved style of expression adopted by their friend and mentor Leigh Hunt. Charles, unsuccessful as a publisher, was eventually (after 1835) much in demand as a lecturer and essayist. Mary, ultimately far more prolific than her husband, earned a special place in literary history for the monumental *Complete Concordance to Shakespeare* (issued in monthly parts, 1844–5), over whose 309,600 entries she laboured, with true Victorian devotion, for sixteen years. But she also wrote poems, novels, short stories, a famous series of fanciful essays *The Girlhood of Shakespeare's Heroines* and, perhaps most surprisingly of all, an elaborate and highly skilled parody of *Hiawatha*. This was published in 1856 under the title *The Song of Drop O'Wather* and the pseudonym Harry Wandsworth Shortfellow. In it she revealed not only a sly sense of humour, but also an unexpected knowledge of London street life and criminal slang:

> Then the nobby Paw-Paw-Keeneyes,
> He the stylish Thimblerigger,
> He the clever sleight-of hander,
> Whom some people called the Black-leg,
> Rose among the guests assembled.
> Skilled he was in sports and pastimes,
> In the hornpipe, named the Sailor's,
> In all games of chance, or cunning;
> Skilled he was in chicken-hazard,
> Cards, and dice, of all description,
> Vingt-et-un, with pool and counters,
> Rouge-et-Noir, the game of sharpers.
> Though the men would call him Swindler,
> Scamp, and Raff, and such-like titles,
> Little heeded he their sneering,
> Little cared he for their chaffing;
> For the women and the damsels
> Favoured stylish Paw-Paw-Keeneyes.
> He was dressed in shirt of cotton,
> Figured large, with pattern showy,
> All stuck down with studs bright gilded;
> He was dressed in white duck trousers,
> Like a cockney out a-boating;
> And he wore his shoes low-quartered,

> Tied with bows and ends that floated;
> On his head was perched a straw hat,
> With blue ribbon knotted round it,
> In his hand he had a switch-cane,
> And a ring upon his finger.[1]

And so it continued for 106 pages, hilariously shadowing every detail of Longfellow's poem.

She also wrote an excellent autobiography, aptly entitled *My Long Life* (1896), and a short account of her father, *The Life and Labours of Vincent Novello* (1864). In collaboration with her husband she edited and added commentaries to Shakespeare's plays. Both worshipped the Bard and were inclined to treat him as a specially favoured member of the family! Their jointly written *Recollections of Writers* (1878) is a mine of entertaining information about the literary scene in which they played so prominent a part.

As a friend of Charles Dickens, Mary also had the pleasure of indulging the Novello delight in theatricals on a specially grand scale when, in 1848, she joined his amateur company in public performances in London, Manchester, Liverpool, Birmingham, Glasgow and Edinburgh. She made a favourable impression as Dame Quickly in *The Merry Wives of Windsor*, and later wrote down the only detailed account of the great adventure.

After Mary Victoria came Joseph Alfred Novello, born in 1810. However his story belongs to a later chapter, for it was he who was responsible for the development of his father's sporadic publications into the wholehearted business concern that is the subject of this book.

Cecilia, born in 1812, studied drama and elocution at Mrs Blaine Hunt's academy, went briefly onto the stage and then succumbed to the charms of the young playwright and poet Thomas James Serle whom she married in 1836. Though according to Macready a 'most amiable man and a very pretty poet',[2] Serle never quite reached the top of his profession, but his home became a meeting place for all the leading writers and actors of the day, and the beautiful Cecilia was its acknowledged queen.

Of all the Novello children, the life of Edward Petre, born in 1813, is surely the most tragic. For, both by the evidence of what his contemporaries said and what he actually managed to achieve in his twenty-three years, he clearly had the makings of an outstanding painter. While still in his teens he attended Henry Sass's famous drawing academy, which gave to Victorian painting such admirable figures as William Frith and Sir John Millais, and then spent three years at the Royal Academy, carrying off the first prize in each successive year. At twenty-one he commenced two years in Paris, working in the Louvre, and had plans for a similar period of study in Italy. But, as his sister Clara recorded:

> Fired and enchanted by all those art treasures, he worked and overworked, and one bitterly cold night, leaving the heated studio where he was studying from the nude, he took violent cold and broke a blood-vessel. Returned home to England, and forced—too late!—to take medical advice, he was put on a starvation regime—he a giant in strength, and of active habits!—and this mistaken treatment killed him...[3]

He left behind portfolios of sketches—some brilliant, some mere journeyman copies of the great masters—and a handful of fine paintings, mostly of his family.

Emma Aloysia, the fifth child, also considered herself a painter, but her talents were not to be compared with those of her brother. Her long life (she lived from 1815 to 1902) was uneventful, save for a tendency towards melancholy and self-reproach which eventually led to her being placed (1882) in an asylum.

Mary Sabilla Novello (1821–1904) also passed a relatively quiet life. To her fell the task of looking after her parents in their old age, and acting as companion and housekeeper to her bachelor brother Alfred. But she was not without talent. She trained successfully as a singer, making, in her younger days, a number of important public appearances. Her treatise, *Voice and Vocal Art*, remained a standard textbook for many years.

The real singer of the family, and in some ways the most remarkable of all the Novello children, was Clara Anastasia (1818–1908). Since music-making was part of the Novello way of life, it is not perhaps surprising that all the children sang. But even from her earliest years it was evident that Clara's response to music was something out of the ordinary. Her ear was acute, her memory exceptional, and her voice had a natural purity. Standing by her father's pianoforte, clutching the dolls she had been playing with, she seemed to find no difficulty in repeating the Handel and Mozart airs he played. At the age of seven she was sent to York, where her brother Alfred was already serving out his time as an apprentice in the music trade, to study with the organist of the Catholic Chapel, John Robinson:

> He gave me rare and short and detested lessons on the pianoforte, hitting my knuckles with a big red pencil he marked fingerings with. I was left for hours daily before the pianoforte, in a room seldom used, and soon I substituted for Cramer's Exercises any vocal music I could run off with from the shelves, and thus I learnt to read and decipher music, never reflecting that my delinquency would be discovered by my voice instead of my fingers being hard at work . . .[4]

In 1828 her parents sought the advice of François Joseph Fétis, the famous French music historian then lecturing in England. He listened amazed as she sang 'The Soldier, tired of War's Alarms' from Dr Arne's opera *Artaxerxes*, sailing effortlessly to its famous top D. He recommended that she should compete for a place in Alexandre Choron's Academy of Classic and Religious Music in Paris. Her parents, already planning a visit to Salzburg to deliver a gift of money to Mozart's sister, seized the opportunity. Clara sang before Choron (and before Rossini the next day) to such effect that it was agreed that despite her age an exception would be made and that she should commence her studies forthwith.

She remained in Paris for two years, leaving somewhat precipitately when the events of the 1830 Revolution disrupted Choron's classes. And then, though scarcely fourteen, she made her public début in October 1832 at a benefit concert in the Theatre Royal, Windsor. 'Her voice', exclaimed the *Windsor and Eton Express*, 'is sweet, and her intonation perfect . . . ultimate great success and fame must be hers'.[5]

And this indeed was what happened. On Christmas Eve the same year she sang the principal soprano part in the first performance in England of Beethoven's *Missa Solemnis* at Thomas Alsager's private music-room. Her father played the organ, and Alfred, Edward and Mary Victoria sang in the choir. By 1833 she was making regular public appearances, including her first Three Choirs Festival (Worcester, 1833). In 1836, after having toured extensively in England and Scotland, she went to Paris to make her continental début. Leipzig followed in 1837, at the special invitation of Mendelssohn, who had heard her sing during his first visit to England and was to remain one of her greatest admirers. A six-month tour then took her to Weimar,

Berlin, Dresden, Vienna, Salzburg and Augsburg, ending in Milan where she was to study operatic technique. Wherever she went she triumphed. By the end of the tour she was not only famous, but also a great deal richer.

It meant that the whole family had gained, for her manager was her indefatigable mother. In Clara Mrs Novello had found rare talent that happened also to be pliant and biddable. Like Leopold Mozart before her, and with the best of intentions, she could not help but exploit the family's good fortune. It does not seem to have occurred to her that her relentless ambition on Clara's behalf bordered on the tyrannical.

A second tour began at the end of 1838, this time to Russia, taking in opportunities at Berlin, Gottingen, Danzig and Königsberg on the way. But it was not a success. The combination of Russian bad manners and bitterly cold weather proved more than either could stand, even for ready money. The return journey, via Düsseldorf and Berlin, did something to restore their humour and their fortunes, but it was a profound relief to be in England once more, singing for the Three Choirs Festival and in hospitable London drawing-rooms.

Clara and her mother returned to Italy in 1840, garnering further triumphs in Germany on the way, and in Milan she settled to a period of intense study. By the following year she had been offered, and had turned down, a contract with La Scala, and in April she began a series of engagements arranged by no less an admirer than Rossini. These included her Italian opera début in Padua on 6 July 1841. Eight performances of *Semiramide* were given to packed houses that cheered themselves hoarse.

Mrs Novello, having arranged that Sabilla should also study in Italy and that Emma should be sent out as a companion to the two sisters, now felt that she could safely leave her daughter to pursue her operatic career. 'Clara', she noted, 'has purchased a very handsome carriage and taken a respectable manservant, so her household is comfortable and elegant for her station'.[6]

For a while everything went as planned. Clara won the approval of critics and audiences alike. On 18 March 1842 she sang, at his special insistence, in the first Italian performance of Rossini's *Stabat Mater*. She was, she observed somewhat ingenuously, 'like a Queen and [I] have my own way in everything'.[7] In August 1842 she went to Fermo to fulfil an engagement to sing Pacini's *Saffo*, and here she began to meet on social terms a young nobleman who had already fallen in love with her from a distance—the twenty-seven-year-old Count Giovanni

Battista Gigliucci. Before the year was out, she too was in love.

Mrs Novello was not pleased. When Clara returned to London in 1843 and the Count presented himself for family approval she refused point blank to acknowledge the possibility of any such marriage. He was, after all, not particularly wealthy–certainly not as wealthy as Clara might hope to be in her own right–and Counts were two a penny in Italy. She 'marvelled', she said, 'at his temerity!'.[8]

But she had forgotten one thing. Clara was her daughter and had inherited the same determined spirit. Moreover, success had given her confidence and she now had no hesitation in asserting her independence. Though the atmosphere in the Novello household was rigid with disapproval, the marriage took place and on 22 November 1843 Clara Novello became the Countess Gigliucci. It meant, of course, that she had to abandon her singing career. But she did so apparently without regret. And there her 'biography' might have ended, were it not for the fact that the Count was actively concerned in Italian politics and the movement to throw off Austrian domination.

The events of that slow progress towards independence and unification came to a first climax in 1849 when the Pope was deposed from his temporal power (he was, however, restored again after only a few months of Republican 'freedom'.) Count Gigliucci, deeply involved, was promptly expelled from the Kingdom of Naples for 'very grave reasons'. Deprived of his sources of income, he was forced, much against his will, to accept Clara's very sensible solution to the whole problem. She would return to the operatic stage.

She sang first in Rome to somewhat indifferent audiences, but gradually she won their approval. Soon other offers began to come in–Florence, Lisbon, and then England. She returned to London in 1851 and commenced the second part of her singing career, rising, so far as the English were concerned, to the highest point of her fame. Here it was mainly as a singer of oratorio that she was admired. The purity of her voice, the effortlessness with which she could soar to the highest notes, the quality of intense spirituality with which she imbued her performances made her the darling of the public. As Madame Clara Novello, the great interpreter of Handel and Mendelssohn, she reigned supreme in their affections.

But events in Italy were also on the move, and by the end of 1860 unification and liberation had been achieved under Victor Emmanuel II. Count Gigliucci was free to return and take his rightful place as a member of the Chamber of Deputies. Obediently, Clara announced her farewell concert, and on 21 November 1860, at the St James's Hall, her matchless voice soared over the choir and orchestra. Critics lamented that her loss to sacred music was 'as great as Malibran's had been to the lyric stage'. There was nobody who could take her place. 'Clara Novello's throne', they declared, 'is empty'.[9]

That Vincent and Mary Novello could have raised so variously talented a family says as much for their abilities as parents as it does for the hereditary factors they brought to their marriage. The omens, of course, were propitious. A mixture of English, Irish, Italian and German blood could scarcely have failed to produce something unusual. Both parents were almost obsessively industrious—idleness to them, was the worst of sins. Both had artistic talent and a degree of creativity which they exercised successfully. Their circle of friends was wide and stimulating, and in no way restricted by creed or social standing. Their opinions were liberal, inclining, even, to radicalism. Their outlook was cosmopolitan. They were, in short, unconventional and thoroughly stimulating.

The Novello attitude to children was, moreover, remarkably enlightened. Always playful with them, they nevertheless treated them seriously. Their children were their friends. They guided their education, conducting much of it themselves, not necessarily formally, but simply by being there to answer questions, share their music and their books, and generally make the process of learning fun. The dead hand of Victorian repression was nowhere to be felt in this essentially eighteenth-century household.

Even allowing for the fact that it would have been hard for a Novello ever to admit that the family was less than perfect, Mary Victoria's account of her childhood is singularly idyllic and affectionate:

The way in which books were made high treats in the Novello family, by the kindly mode of their bringing, furnishes pleasant and salutary example for other young fathers and mothers rearing a family on slender pecuniary resources. Often, when late overnight professional avocations made early rising an impossibility to Vincent Novello, he would have his young ones brought on the bed while he ate the breakfast his wife brought him, and showed them some delightful volume he had purchased as a present for them. First came the "looking at the pictures"; then, the multiplicity of eager enquiry they elicited; then, the explanation; then, the telling of the subject of the book; then, the account of its author; then, the final glory of seeing *V. Novello's children, 240, Oxford Street*, written in the blank leaf, or cover, at the beginning. After this fashion were 'Aesop's Fables', 'Lamb's Tales from Shakespeare', 'Sandford and Merton', 'Maria Edgeworth's Early Lessons and Parents' Affidavit', 'Priscilla Wakefield's Juvenile Travellers', 'The Hundred Wonders of the World', and 'The Book of Trades', successively brought home and enjoyed. The due intermixture of practicality and imagination in the works chosen for and given to their children, serve to indicate the judgment evinced by Vincent and Mary Novello in eliciting and cherishing the various biases in their boys' and girls' several faculties.[10]

Even visits to the theatre, which Vincent Novello adored and which many parents of the time would have considered morally dangerous, were allowed as special treats:

Some of these theatre-treats remain still as bright points in "the dark backward and abysm of time" to the remembrance of Vincent Novello's children. Once, riding home on his shoulder, tired and sleepy, after the glory of going "to see the play"; so young was then the rememberer, so kind was the good father. Once a wondrous night of fine-cast comedy, when Munden played Old Dornton; Elliston, young Dornton; Terry, Sulky; Knight, Silky; Mrs Harlowe and Miss Kelly the Widow and the Spinster, in "The Road to Ruin": and when the farce was "The Turnpike Gate", with Munden as Crack, the Cobbler. Once, a night of joyful surprise, when the father, coming home tired with a long day's school-teaching, bade his little girl get Shakespeare's play of "Much Ado about Nothing", and read him the opening scenes while he ate his dinner (which she had prepared, laying the cloth for Papa, as Mamma was upstairs with the new baby); and then, as a reward for his daughter's good housewifery, telling her to put on her bonnet and he would take her to Covent Garden Theatre, to see Charles Kemble play Benedick.[11]

Memories of their Oxford Street childhood, so near the open country in those days, remained in Mary Victoria's mind, bathed in a touching glory:

The early market-carts that rumbled by of a morning, with their supply of fresh vegetables and fruit, bringing a delicious air from . . . the lanes and fields . . . But even Hyde Park, where I was entrusted to convoy my younger brothers and sisters, supplied me with enjoyment of those fine old elm trees, those stretches of grass I beheld. Such things as halfpenny little mugs of curds and whey were extant in those days—sold near to the Park entrance, then called Cumberland Gate, now known as the Marble Arch . . . The railing adjacent to the gate was, at that period, permitted to be strung with rows of printed old-fashioned ballads, such as "Cruel Barbara Allen" . . .

There was a small stationery shop in Quebec Street, kept by a Miss Lavoine, where we children bought slates and slate-pencils; and a certain bakery in Bryanston Street that had a curved iron railing below its shop window, which tempted us to spend some of our pocket money in pennyworths of old-world gingerbread figure-cakes, in the shape of lions, tigers, horses, dogs, cocks and hens, castles, alphabets and other objects, besides selling crisp squares of "parliament", crunched by us with considerable satisfaction . . .

Another of our urban delights in those days was watching, from the window of our front-parlour nursery, "the soldiers" as they passed from the barracks in Portman Street to parade in Hyde Park. First came a magnificent and imperious drum-major, who, notwithstanding the importance with which he wielded his tall staff of office, seeming solemnly to pick his way with it, used to cast a smiling eye toward the group of young faces that peered admiringly over the low, green blind at him and his brilliant troop preceded by its band of music.

One of the chief figures among these was a black man, who brandished and clashed a pair of dazzling cymbals; and another was also a black, who upheld a kind of oriental standard that had horse tails dangling therefrom, and jingling bells pendant from a central silver crescent . . . [Such memories] add brilliancy to those mornings, and strengthen the contrast they afford with the dimness of the previous evenings, for Oxford Street was then lighted at night by oil lamps, gas lighting not being invented.

Opposite to our house was Camelford House, where Prince Leopold and Princess Charlotte resided when in town, . . . Once I saw her going to Court, the indispensable hoop tilted sideways to enable her to take her seat in the carriage, and the equally indispensable huge plume of feathers then required for Court costume. When her early death threw all England into mourning –for no one, however poor, but had at least a scrap of crape about them–my father set to music Leigh Hunt's touching verses,– "His departed love to Prince Leopold." . . . .

An enchanting treat of those childish years was that we called 'a day in the fields'. Our place of assembling was generally some spot between Hampstead and Highgate (no Regent's Park or Zoological Gardens then in existence!) and there we met, by appointment, Leigh Hunt and his family, the Gliddons and their families, our company being often enhanced in brightness by the advent from town of lively Henry Robinson and ever-young Charles Cowden Clarke. The picnic part of our entertainment was cold lamb and salad prepared by my mother, she being an acknowledged adept in the dressing of this latter.[12]

And there they would read plays and poems, make up puns and comic verse, until at last it was time to bring out the four volumes of glees and part-songs, elegantly bound in green leather and entitled *Music for the Open Air*, which Vincent Novello had copied out for family entertainment on just such occasions.

Wrapped in mutual affection, emotionally secure and intellectually stimulated, it is little wonder that the Novello children grew to be a close-knit family. Had they needed a motto it would undoubtedly have run to the tune 'The Family is All', for this was the principle which guided their lives and which provided the firm foundation upon which their later publishing activities were to be built.

CHAPTER THREE

THE FIRM ESTABLISHED

The first Novello publication was, as we have seen, a two-volume collection of sacred music, 'composed, selected and arranged' by Vincent Novello, and issued in May 1811.[1] Whether it can truly be said to mark the beginning of the publishing house is a matter of opinion. So far as Vincent himself was concerned it was a private venture, backed by the pledges of 301 subscribers, headed by the Dukes of Kent, Cambridge and Gloucester, and the Princesses Mary and Sophia, with a total of 472 copies (of which a Revd O'Moran of Dublin laid claim to no fewer than 100!). Prominent among the musicians who subscribed were Thomas Attwood, Dr Charles Burney, Muzio Clementi, William Hawes, William Shield, Thomas Walmisley and the Webbes, senior and junior. Each subscriber promised a guinea; non-subscribers would have to pay an extra five shillings for their lack of faith. The whole was decently printed by Phipps & Co., Duke Street, Grosvenor Square, who designed a particularly elegant title page in several ornamental type-faces and much scroll-work. The preface is worth considering:

> Most of the following Pieces were written at different intervals for the sole use of the Portuguese Chapel and without any view to future Publication; but from their having been found not ill-adapted to the Powers of a small Choir, and more particularly in consequence of the very great scarcity of similar productions; so many applications were made from Persons who were desirous

of possessing Copies, that I at last resolved to alter my original intention and to publish them.

In order to afford Variety (by contrast with the simplicity of my own little compositions) and at the same time to give real value to the Collection, I have selected & inserted some of the most approved Pieces from the masterly productions of Mozart, Haydn, Durante, &c,—Several of these however in their original state were so very long, that it would have been impossible to have performed them, without extending the duration of the service to an unusual and inconvenient length. As the only alternative therefore was abridgement, or total omission, I preferred the former, and ventured to curtail and alter some of the movements, so as to reduce them within the customary limits.

It was suggested that it would be better to publish all the Vocal Parts (except the Bass) in the Treble Clef, but as I consider this practice as an innovation, I was unwilling to afford an additional example of an erroneous custom that has already become too prevalent. The Treble Clef when applied to the Counter Tenor & Tenor parts does not indicate the real or true notes that are required to be sung. The C Clef does, and I trust therefore that no Apology is necessary on my part for preferring Truth to Falsehood, or that which is proper to that which is improper.

In forming this Collection, my principal object has been, in the first place, to render it of general utility in Catholic Choirs, by selecting those Pieces, the words of which most frequently form part of the Public Service, & in the Second place, by endeavouring to combine variety of style with facility of execution, to render it acceptable to those Amateurs who occasionally dedicate the Sunday Evening to the performance of Sacred Music in Private.[2]

Apart from the strictures about clefs, which Vincent was soon to drop, and the concentration on music for exclusively Catholic choirs, the Novello approach to music publishing was to remain unchanged: to make good music accessible and easy to perform.

The preface, however, makes no reference to an important innovation mentioned, almost casually, on the title page. Vincent Novello had provided his scores with a fully realized accompaniment instead of the figured bass customary at the time. Not everyone appreciated his thoughtfulness. Professional musicians were annoyed that the veil of secrecy had been lifted from an important part of their craft. At this rate they might soon be out of a job! But the Novello example proved infectious, and soon it became common for all scores to be printed in this way.

Three major publications followed during the next eleven years. First, *A Collection of Motetts for the Offertory*, issued in twelve books, or two bound volumes; second, in 1816, *Twelve Easy Masses for Small Choirs*, in three volumes; and finally, in 1822, *The Evening Service* ('a collection of pieces appropriate to Vespers, Compline & Tenebrae, including the whole of the Gregorian Hymns for every principal festival throughout the year'), again issued in twelve books, or two volumes.[3]

Though the Novello family changed address several times during this period, moving from Oxford Street to 8 Percy Street, near Bedford Square, in 1820, and to Shacklewell Green in 1823, there seems to have been no attempt to set up business premises. Indeed, the move to Shacklewell Green in remote and rural Hackney suggests the very opposite.

At this point in his life Vincent had reasons for seeking a more peaceful existence. He no longer played at the Portuguese Embassy Chapel (the building itself was soon to be pulled down) so he was now in a position to relax his teaching practice and bury himself in musical research, with a view to future publication. On a more personal level, he had been shattered by the death of his young son, Sydney Vincent, in 1820. The boy, scarcely four years old, had died after a fall. Vincent's attachment had, we are told, 'something of an exclusive fondness about it, that rendered it different from his affection towards his other children'.[4] From then onwards he became increasingly a prey to periods of depression from which nothing could shake him:

> So long as this sombre visitation lasted, a deep melancholy settled upon [his] mind, and deprived him of all powers of taking pleasure in life, family, friends or pursuits. Even his beloved Art, his adored Music, ceased to have interest for him; and it was only mechanically, and as a mere matter of principle, that he fulfilled his professional duties.[5]

If the move to Shacklewell Green was made partly in the hope that a more relaxed, country kind of life would help to ease his spirits, there seems also to have been an additional motive–economy. His friends were appalled. It was, complained Leigh Hunt, a 'dull, doleful, damnable place', a 'huddled nest of sixteen rooms, low & small' surrounded by 'a dismal garden & a damp arbour'.[6] But in the end they consented to make the journey and the old, convivial meetings continued as before. And to at least one child, the five-year-old Clara, it was a very heaven:

> The house in Shacklewell formed the corner of the "Green", and stood in its own gardens–a small front one, and beyond the entrance gate, a row of shady lime-trees. At the back of the house, called "The Cottage"–such a sweet, rural sound!–was a somewhat larger garden, flanked by big trees, in one of which hung a swing. Beyond, was a large fruit orchard, and my favourite resort was its cherry tree, up which I soon climbed, and used to lie at length on its cross branches, which made quite a luxurious couch, dreaming of deserts and forests . . .[7]

Vincent may also have had other problems on his mind at this time. A letter from Charles Lamb to Leigh Hunt, written in 1825, hints, behind the banter, at a degree of religious wavering:

> I was with the Novellos last week. They have a large, cheap house and garden, with a dainty library (magnificent) without books. But what will make you bless yourself (I am too old for wonder), something has touched the right organ in Vincentio at last. He attends a Wesleyan chapel on Kingsland Green. He at first tried to laugh it off–he only went for the singing; but the cloven hoof–I retract–the Lamb's trotters–are at length apparent. Mary Isabella [Mrs Novello] attributes it to a lightness induced by his headaches. But I think I see in it a less accidental influence. Mister [Cowden] Clark[e] is at perfect staggers! the whole fabric of his infidelity is shaken. He has no one to join him in his coarse insults and indecent obstreperousnesses against Christianity, for Holmes (the bonny Holmes) is gone to Salisbury to be organist, and Isabella and the Clarke[e] make but a feeble quorum. The children have all nice, neat little clasped pray-books, and I have laid out 7s 8d in *Watts's Hymns* for Christmas presents for them. The eldest girl alone holds out: she has been at Boulogne, skirting upon the vast focus of Atheism, and [has] imported bad principles in patois French. But the

strongholds are crumbling. N. appears as yet to have but a confused notion of the Atonement. It makes him giddy, he says, to think much about it.[8]

There is, in fact, considerable evidence to suggest that Vincent took his Catholicism in a very natural, undogmatic way. 'He as much merits the title of one of the "faithful" (in the Roman Catholic sense, which always signifies a bigoted Papist) as you or I', wrote his blunt friend Samuel Wesley in July 1816, 'for he believes not a word of Purgatory, Priestly Absolution, Transubstantiation, Extreme Unction nor any other extreme of such extreme absurdities'.[9] Many of his closest friends were decidedly liberal in their religious views, and one at least (the poet Shelley) was an avowed atheist. What mattered to Vincent Novello was that they were all good men and true, whose joyful reverence for life surpassed the limitations of mere doctrine.

His son, Joseph Alfred, seems also to have refused the rigours of Catholic precepts. On 9 May 1835, at a time when membership was proscribed by the Vatican on pain of excommunication, he became a Freemason, being admitted to the third degree (Master Mason) in the St Thomas Lodge no. 166, London, on 4 November the same year. That he was also elected a Freeman of the City of London on 6 February 1845, rather suggests that business interests came first in his scale of priorities. It should be remembered that Catholicism was by no means popular, even by this time. There were anti-Catholic riots in London as late as 1850. A cheerful pragmatism would have been by far the best stance for an ambitious young businessman. Indeed, a letter from his mother, dated 12 October 1840, could even be interpreted to mean that he had changed his allegiance altogether. She writes: 'You will pay the rent and taxes for papa, if he wishes it, to save him all popish trouble . . . '.[10] The Novello family seem to have had a very relaxed attitude to religion.

Despite his bouts of melancholia, and possible religious uncertainties, Vincent Novello's plans for publications continued to grow more ambitious. The year 1825 marked the beginning of a major undertaking: the publication of vocal scores of no fewer than eighteen masses by Mozart, and sixteen by Haydn, together with the necessary orchestral material for their proper performance. Hitherto, rather less than half this number had been available to the general public, and then only in full scores printed abroad without the separate organ accompaniment that he now provided. To accomplish this project he had drawn upon manuscript copies hidden away in libraries and private collections, including some obtained from Prince Esterházy himself.

The same year saw the publication of an equally remarkable set of five volumes, each containing a selection of important Italian works from the manuscript collection in the Fitzwilliam Museum, which the Cambridge University authorities had asked him to examine and report upon in 1824. Music by Bononcini, Carissimi, Durante, Jomelli, Vittoria, Orlando di Lasso, Palestrina, Pergolesi and Stradella was included in the collection; and if, by present-day standards, the editorial method may seem somewhat cavalier, the sheer bravado of the undertaking, not to mention the enormous industry involved in transcribing each piece by hand (in fact he published only about a third of what he actually copied out), is a staggering tribute to Vincent Novello's courage and musical perception.

What followed was even more remarkable. In December 1828 he commenced publication of *Purcell's Sacred Music*, a collection eventually completed in October 1832, running to five volumes and issued originally as seventy-two numbers. The music had been gathered in from many different sources, including the library of York Minster where, during the music festival of 1828, he had copied out four anthems and the Evening Service in G minor shortly before the library and organ were destroyed by fire (2 February 1829). The music would have been lost but for Vincent's copies.

The Purcell collection was the first music outside the Roman Rite that he had published, and with it he may be said to have taken the decisive step into publishing on a commercial basis. If what he had set in motion as, virtually, a mere hobby was to continue and grow, it must now have been obvious that a completely new attitude would have to be adopted. Fortunately there were two people who could help him. One was his wife, whose ambition and energetic practicality set the whole process in motion. The other was his son, Joseph Alfred Novello.

In the summer of 1830, when the house of Novello came into existence, Joseph Alfred, or J. Alfred Novello as he came to be known, was not quite twenty. After perfecting his French at M Bonnefoy's Academy near Boulogne ('children to receive a good education, blended with every care and tenderness of domestic treatment'),[11] he had been apprenticed to the 'music seller and music teacher', John Robinson of York. His indentures, dated 17 May 1824, spell out, in the customary apocalyptic terms, what was expected in those days of a fourteen-year-old boy on five years' probation:

The said Apprentice his said Master well and faithfully shall serve, his Secrets shall keep, his lawful Commands shall do, Fornication or Adultery shall not commit, Hurt or Damage to his said Master shall not do, or consent to be done, but to the utmost of his power shall prevent it, and forthwith his said Master shall thereof warn: Taverns or Ale-houses he shall not haunt or frequent, unless it be about his Master's business there to be done: At Dice, Cards, Tables, Bowls, or any other unlawful Games he shall not play: the Goods of his Master he shall not waste nor them lend, or give to any Person without his Master's licence: Matrimony within the said term shall not contract . . . [12]

And whether by temperament so inclined, or merely by virtue of the powerful warning, Joseph Alfred Novello never did, so far as anything of his life is known, commit any of these offences.

He proved, in fact, to be an unusual mixture of business acumen and personal meekness. His devotion to his mother was intense. A brief quotation from a letter written on 15 July 1848 (he was thirty-eight) may serve to show the depth of his feeling:

Often in the watches of the night, Dear Mother, our spirits meet I doubt not; for [so] often in that tranquil time do my thoughts rest upon your beloved image that it must needs be that some soul-sympathy takes actual effect . . . [13]

In taking over his father's business in 1830 and devoting the next thirty years to turning it into a major publishing house, there can be little doubt that Joseph Alfred Novello was acting out his mother's ambitions—just as Clara was to do through her singing.

The precise nature of the arrangement he came to with his father is not known. It would seem likely, however, that the success of his earlier publications enabled Vincent to put up a capital sum to launch the business. A letter written by Mrs Novello to her son on 12 October 1840 would seem to confirm that some such arrangement had been reached: 'As regards the interest of £2,000 from the business, that must depend upon your convenience. You can give Papa some money on account and pay the rest when convenient to you'. [14]

The tone of voice also suggests that she was the driving force behind the enterprise and that by this time Vincent had almost been relegated to the position of sleeping partner.

Money may also have been put up by Charles Cowden Clarke and certain family friends. There seems to have been a general tendency to pool resources, and there are frequent references in their letters to 'The Funds'. For example, Miss Betsy Hill, who had looked after Clara in York, made over the sum of £500 to Alfred (and left it to him in her will) in return for a guaranteed income for life.

Whatever the details of the arrangement, the fact that in 1830 both parents were prepared to stake everything on the abilities of their nineteen-year-old son says much for their attitude to life in general and their family in particular. What brought them to their decision is not known, though in 1829 they had had plenty of time to draw breath and appraise the future. In June that year they embarked upon an extended tour of the continent.

Their destination was Salzburg, and with them they carried a purse containing sixty guineas collected by sixteen London admirers of Mozart 'for the purpose of offering a small present to the Sister of Mozart, as a trifling token of their respect for the memory of her illustrious Brother, and of their cordial sentiments towards his estimable Sister, Madame Sonnenburg'.[15]

The journey, which took them to Antwerp, Cologne, Mannheim, Heidelberg, Stuttgart, Munich, Salzburg, Linz and Vienna, and then back via Strasbourg and Paris, has been amply recorded in *A Mozart Pilgrimage*, compiled by Nerina Medici and Rosemary Hughes from the diaries that Vincent and Mary kept (Vincent reported on his musical impressions, taking notes for a Mozart biography he had in mind, while Mary kept a critical eye open on more general matters). The result is a delightful and totally absorbing picture of music in Europe as seen by two enthusiastic, but level-headed, members of the English bourgeoisie.

For the sidelights it throws on Mozart, as remembered by his family and friends, and the touching account of his sister in her old age, it is invaluable. A brief extract from Vincent's diary, dated Monday, 15 July 1829, may serve to suggest its unique flavour:

A still more delightful day, if possible, than yesterday–Mozart's son came to me about 11 to conduct us to his aunt Sonnenburg. After a little chat we accompanied him to her house, which was within a few yards of where we resided. It seems that she had passed a very restless and sleepless night for fear that we should not come to see her, and had repeatedly expressed her regret that we had not been admitted when we first called. On entering the room, the sister of Mozart was reclining placidly in bed—but blind, feeble, and nearly speechless. Her nephew kindly explained who we were, and she seemed to derive much gratification from the intelligence we conveyed to her. During the whole time, I held her poor thin hand in mine...[16]

The Novellos returned to England towards the end of August 1829, and presumably set about putting their plans for Alfred's future into action. In the years immediately preceding the Salzburg pilgrimage the family had been restless. The house at Shacklewell Green had been succeeded, in 1826, by a town house at 22 Bedford Square, Covent Garden, and this in turn had given way to one at 66 Great Queen Street, Lincoln's Inn. They now proposed to move to a commercially more advantageous area, and accordingly, in March 1830, packed their belongings once more and took up residence at 67 Frith Street.

The shop, if such it can be called, was modest: 'a couple of parlour-windows and a glass-door, with a few title-pages bearing composers' names of sterling merit, and Vincent Novello's as editor...'.[17] Alfred was to promote the business, and Vincent to guide the choice of music they were to handle.

The most immediate task was the continuation and completion of the Purcell collection. It is interesting to note that only sixty-two subscribers could be found to underwrite this particular venture, such was the state of Purcell's 'popularity' at this period, and such the measure of courage involved in the undertaking.

The early Novello publications, all printed by outside firms, were mainly in folio, some, for example the Haydn and Mozart masses, in an oblong format. Besides the complete vocal score, individual voice parts were printed (an innovation not much liked by choirs). Prices varied, but the Haydn and Mozart masses were offered from 2s to 9s 6d according to size. At the time this was thought to be a dangerously low price, prejudicial, even, to the dignity of music. But the Novellos were to go much further in this direction.

Released from the tedium of seeing publications through the printer, Vincent Novello's own musical activities took on a new lease of life in the 1830s. His glee *Old May Morning* was awarded the

Manchester Prize in 1832, and on 17 March 1834 the Philharmonic Society gave the first performance of *Rosalba*, a cantata he composed at their special request. Novellos figured prominently on that occasion at the Hanover Square Rooms with Vincent conducting and Clara and Alfred singing the principal parts. Though heavily influenced by Handel and Mozart, the music is more than competent: the melodies have great charm with even a touch of passion, and the harmony is handled with considerable resource.

Much the same can be said of the composition by which he became best known, and which was composed in 1831: the recitative and song, *The Infant's Prayer*, to words by Mrs Novello. In view of the infants they themselves had lost, it is not perhaps surprising to find that it is something of a tear-jerker:

> May length of days, with honour crown'd,
> On earth their portion be;
> And smiling Cherubs whisper peace,
> When Death their souls sets free.[18]

It went on to sell more than 70,000 copies during his lifetime, and was still in print at the time of World War I.

At this time Vincent Novello also became involved in the activities of two important groups of amateur singers: the City of London Classical Harmonists, founded in 1831, and the Choral Harmonists who succeeded them in 1833. Though both were devoted to the performance of great choral music, the Harmonists operated on a larger scale with full orchestra and choir and professional soloists. They met, agreeably enough, at the London Tavern, and Vincent frequently acted as their conductor.

In 1834 it was found necessary to move the publishing business to 69 Dean Street. As in Frith Street, the family lived over the shop, but now the premises were rather more spacious and convenient. It was a house that at various times had given shelter to the 4th Viscount Castle-comer, Sir John Wynn, the Hon Baron Grant, Sir Lionel Darell and Sir Thomas Bell, and it was to be the Novello headquarters for thirty-three years. It remained part of their empire until 1898, and it is still possible, in certain lights and from certain angles, to discern their name beneath the paintwork. In recent years, however, it has catered for the tastes of a very different kind of client.

By 1837 the business had expanded so healthily that the family decided to move out altogether and give over the whole of the Dean Street building to its needs. They (Vincent and Mary Novello, Charles and Mary Cowden Clarke, Joseph Alfred, and any other Novello child that happened to be in need of a London bed at the time) set up home first at 4 Craven Hill, and then a few yards off in no. 9–a house they preferred to call 'Craven Cottage'. Though within easy walking distance of Dean Street, Craven Hill presented an almost rural aspect, Bayswater being then a leafy suburb of apple orchards and cherry trees. It was to be their last important London home.

As the business expanded and J. Alfred Novello began to be more and more adventurous in his publishing policy, it would seem that Vincent turned increasingly to scholarly pursuits: copying manuscripts, digging up forgotten treasures, editing and arranging his finds to suit the nineteenth-century amateur's tastes and abilities. The day-to-day running of the firm he left entirely to his son.

Few letters relating to business matters survive from this period, but one, written from Berlin on 29 April 1839 while Mrs Novello was furthering Clara's career, gives more than a hint that an uneasy situation had arisen between father and son:

> My blessing ever rest upon you dearest Alf for your obedience, and good temper under disagreeables that will arise in the most united families. Your dear father is no judge of business, never was, and I always dreaded his meddling with affairs out of his art... I wish dear Papa would settle the *business* upon you and me, Alf–we would divide the profits and pay him handsomely for his *original* compositions and arrangements of what *we should choose*. I must talk to him when I get him over to Düsseldorf...
>
> God bless you my dear boy–write if you can–post the letter to Düsseldorf, mention the money and keep nothing secret from me, or I cannot act. I know it is home policy to keep disagreeables from me, lest I fret–but do not, and I may advise.
>
> Blessings attend you, prays your loving friend and mother
> Mary Sabilla Novello.[19]

In the end it seems that by 1840 it was necessary to dissolve the formal partnership. Vincent continued to edit and compose as vigorously as ever, but it is significant that at least a handful of his works were issued by other publishers. In 1842, for example, Monro & May brought out his collection of *Sixty Italian Rounds*, while in 1845 Coventry & Hollier appear as publishers of his *Studies in Vocal Counterpoint*. It would seem that once Alfred had assumed sole command he reserved the right to be more particular about which of his father's enthusiasms he chose to endorse.

Letters of this period also rather suggest that Vincent, perhaps because of his depressions, had grown rather suspicious and difficult. One to Dr Rimbault, dated 12 June 1845, refers to several volumes of Dr Blow's anthems which were to be collected at Dean Street:

> As this is not the first time that I have detected the shop-people in Dean St in taking the liberty of not only detaining parcels belonging to me, but of *suppressing* messages that have been left there for me, I have *forbidden them from taking charge of anything of mine*, or of meddling in any way with parcels, or letters, addressed to me, for the future.[20]

Another, to Joseph Alfred (16 January 1849), suggests that he did not age well:

> I am very much vexed and offended to find that I have been deprived of the power of selling out any of the money which belongs to me in the Funds, without the necessity of going through a troublesome, boring set of formalities that are as annoying to my spirit of independence and accustomed unshackled freedom of will and action as they are totally *unexpected* and disagreeable as forming impediments and restraints upon the mode of conduct I choose to pursue. When I consented to the introduction of my wife's name, in addition to my own, with reference to the property belonging to me in the Funds, I intended to give her the power of dispersing of it in my absence, and independently of me, if she wished to do so; but I did *not* intend to *deprive myself* of the power of doing the same, in her absence, if I wished ever to do so![21]

The last years of Vincent and Mary Novello are soon told and are somewhat less absorbing. There were, of course, moments when the old fire asserted itself. In 1837, for example, there was the excitement of entertaining Mendelssohn once more, and the anticipation of seeing him conduct *St Paul* at the Birmingham Festival. For months the family had listened to detailed accounts of the new combination stops that Vincent had invented for the great organ that William Hill was building in Birmingham's town hall. Moreover, he was to go there himself to play at the *St Paul* concert. But, almost at the last moment, he was overcome by depression and refused to make the journey.

His mood must have steadied by 1840, for in that year he undertook regular duties as organist again, this time at the Roman Catholic Chapel in Moorfields (the Pro-Cathedral for London). He also composed incidental music ('solemn and affecting strains', according to the dramatist[22]) for the Covent Garden production of Leigh Hunt's poetic drama *A Legend of Florence*. When the young Queen Victoria attended the play for a second time, Hunt seems to have spent more of the occasion observing the royal reaction than watching the play, for he records with satisfaction that 'when the lovely organ strain, composed by my friend Vincent Novello, began to double the tears of the audience, a fair hand was observed to come from behind the royal curtain, and press the congenial arm next to it, as if in affecting remembrance' (the 'congenial arm' being presumably that of Prince Albert of Saxe-Coburg).[23]

By 1848 matters were again less happy. Mrs Novello was now far from well, and it was decided that she should live in a warmer climate. Alfred duly took a lease on an apartment in a charming villa set deep in the hills to the east of Nice, overlooking the bay. And here at the Villa Quaglia, accompanied by her daughter Sabilla, Mary Novello retired to live out her days.

Not that she was inactive. The year 1848 had already seen the composition of a song by Vincent to her words in praise of Italy and designed to further Garibaldi's cause:

> Assist them, Lord! their chains to rive,
> Attend their fervent Patriot cries:
> Deliver them from foreign thrall,
> Let envious, rival factions cease;
> Reward their sacrifice and toil
> With Liberty and lasting Peace![24]

(In much the same spirit Sabilla Novello had arranged a bunch of national songs into an 'Anti-Corn-Law-League Quadrille' for the great Anti-Corn-Law Bazaar of 1845, in which all the Novellos figured vociferously.)

Vincent, Alfred and the Cowden Clarkes visited Nice in the spring of 1849, and, finding that Mrs Novello's health was so much improved, it was decided that Vincent should join her permanently and that the Villa Quaglia should become a second Novello home. By 1852 he must have become completely reconciled to the change, for on 25 June Messrs Puttick & Simpson offered part of his musical library for sale in their Piccadilly auction rooms. Parcelled out in 367 lots, it amounted to some eight hundred volumes, including manuscripts of J. C. Bach and Samuel Wesley. The catalogue reads as a fascinating testimony to the breadth of his taste and curiosity, and the depth of his scholarship.

Warmed by regular visits from the family, including Clara and the grandchildren (Count Gigliucci had by now been forgiven), Vincent and Mary's last years passed pleasantly enough. For her the end came suddenly. After only a few hours' illness she died of cholera on 25 July 1854.

She remained in character to the last. Only a few days before her death she drafted a letter 'To the Working Classes of Great Britain'. Whether she posted it, and whether it was ever printed, we do not know; but its style and content are typical of the values that guided her through life. The good intentions, the steadfast belief in industry and self-improvement and the fatal touch of self-righteousness are all there:

My dear Countrymen and Countrywomen,
    Though forced myself to live during my old age in a warmer climate than England, yet my heart is with you and interested in your welfare. It was with great sorrow I read of the protracted strike last winter, for all your sakes: believe me that the only method to acquire your just demands, is by earnest remonstrance with your employers, and reforming your *own* social habits; thereby proving you are worthy of a more advanced position in society. Labour whilst in health, and during youth and manhood, is the portion of all mankind and it develops our bodily and mental faculties and has been deemed by wise man an acceptable prayer to God. Clever men have been of the opinion that National Songs are calculated to develop and improve the moral condition of the people and convey many useful lessons in a pleasant manner: most of us recollect the popularity and moral tendency of Dibdin's songs, and the benefit they conferred upon seafaring men. Without pretending to his talents I have ventured

to write one [such song] for the Spinners, who appear to me reflective beings capable of much improvement, and a second for the Pittmen, whose labour is so essential to others. I have touched upon a tender point that man should be the 'Bread Winner' for his family, whilst wives should work at home, rendering it comfortable, neat and pleasant, and without this arrangement there can be no domestic happiness: husbands will frequent beer shops, and wives will become slatternly gossips, whilst children are neglected. There will always be single women sufficient for the work of a mill, whilst married women are more usefully occupied in the discharge of their housewifely duties. Should my attempts please those for whom they were written and afford them one moral or pleasant thought, I shall be highly rewarded in my humble *foreign* cot.

Mary Sabilla Novello[25]

Perhaps Vincent, or one of the children, managed to persuade her that a miner's song with the refrain 'Lumpity, lump!' might not seem as appropriate in the Yorkshire coal fields as it did in Nice?

Vincent himself lived for seven more years, looked after by Alfred and the Cowden Clarkes, first at 27 Porchester Terrace, and then, after 1856, in Nice when Alfred retired. He died on 9 August 1861, a few weeks short of his eightieth birthday.

Such were the services he had rendered to music in general, and British music in particular, that it was deemed only fitting that he, a Roman Catholic, should be honoured with a memorial window in Westminster Abbey, in the North Transept, close to Poets' Corner and the seat in which it had been his custom to sit when he came 'to hear the anthem'.[26] It was destroyed in an air raid in 1941, but a national appeal, headed by Lord Harewood, Sir John Barbirolli, Sir Malcolm Sargent, Sir Arthur Bliss, and the poet T. S. Eliot, was launched in November 1961 and in due course it was replaced by a fine chamber organ, constructed from two Snetzler organs of the mid-eighteenth century.

CHAPTER FOUR

JOSEPH ALFRED NOVELLO

A circular, elegantly printed on quarto-sized paper, fixes the date of Alfred Novello's entry into the business world as 'Midsummer, 1830'. He was then a few weeks short of his twentieth birthday (12 August) and pleasantly filled with all the enthusiasm and optimism of youth:

> MR JOSEPH ALFRED NOVELLO respectfully informs the Nobility, Gentry, and the Public in general, that he has just opened an Establishment, at No 67, FRITH STREET, *one door from Soho Square*, for the sale of his Father's Works and other Musical Publications of every class; all kinds of Instruments, Roman and Silver'd Violin and Harp Strings of the very best quality, and all other articles connected with the Musical business.
>
> He has ventured to annex a Catalogue of his Publications, and he flatters himself that, by his strict attention and punctuality in the fulfilment of any order with which he may be favoured, he shall prove himself worthy of the kind patronage and encouragement of his friends.[1]

The business, it appears, was set up as a general music shop and not simply as a publishing house. A later advertisement[2] makes it clear that at this stage in its development all kinds of things were grist to the Novello mill:

GRAND, CABINET, AND SQUARE PIANO FORTES
BY THE BEST MAKERS,
AND ALL SORTS OF MUSICAL INSTRUMENTS.
N.B. EMINENT QUADRILLE PLAYERS PROVIDED
FOR BALLS.

The same advertisement states that the firm was also the 'Manu-facturer of Silver'd String on a Peculiar and Improved Plan, which prevents the Wires ever relaxing from the String'–a hint, perhaps, that the young Alfred had already begun to demonstrate the skills as an inventor that were to dominate his years of retirement. Later we find the firm advertising Vincent Novello's advice in the construction and installation of organs, and offering its premises as the meeting place of Sabilla Novello's singing classes ('for young ladies'), and even as the location of Mr James Theobald's 'Foreign Wine Cellars' ('Very Superior Port and Sherry' could be 'drawn from the wood at 14s per gallon, or 28s per dozen and upwards')![3]

But even without these attractions there was every reason to suppose the venture would be a success. Vincent was at the top of his profession, known to, and well-liked by his contemporaries. His name on any music score, whether as composer or editor, was a guarantee of excellence. Clara, though a mere twelve-year-old, was about to commence her career as a singer (1831) and could therefore be relied upon not only to exploit Novello publications but to add lustre to their name wherever she went–a living and very potent advertisement. Alfred himself possessed a fine bass voice and, like Clara, could carry the Novello message wherever he sang in public. Mary Victoria, recently married to Charles Cowden Clarke, was available for literary advice; and her husband was not averse to lending a hand with the firm's business. Even Vincent's pupil the musical historian Edward Holmes, who, in typical Novello fashion, had spent several years living in with the family and had taken Mrs Novello as a travelling companion on his 1827 tour of musical Germany, was there to contribute. And above all, advising and encouraging, bullying and cajoling, was Mary Sabilla herself. In short, the entire family, and many of its friends, was geared to making the new firm a success.

At first it was Vincent's ideas that dominated the publishing policy. The five-volume edition of Purcell's sacred music was completed in October 1832, and was followed by a collection of pieces for female voices, entitled *Convent Music*–a very singular enterprise for those days. Then came *The Psalmist* (a collection of psalm and hymn tunes 'adapted as well for Social and Domestic Devotion as for Public Worship'), and *The Congregational and Choristers' Psalm and Hymn Book*. On a more ambitious scale, preparations were made to issue two-volume collections of anthems by William Croft and Maurice Greene, with those of William Boyce to follow in four volumes.

The influence of Alfred's taste begins to make itself felt in August 1832, with the publication of the first book of Mendelssohn's *Songs Without Words* issued under the title: *Original Melodies for the Piano Forte*. Though by now Mendelssohn had become a close friend of the family, meeting them probably during his first visit to England in 1829, the firm still felt unable to proceed with his music entirely at their own risk. The pieces were therefore published 'for the author', with the profits split on a fifty-fifty basis. Mendelssohn cheerfully informed his friend Ignaz Moscheles that the work would 'certainly go through at least twenty editions, and with the proceeds I shall buy the house No 2 Chester Place [Moscheles lived at no. 3], and a seat in the House of Commons, and become a Radical by profession'.[4] After ten months, however, he had to be content with £4 16s 0d–the half share on forty-eight copies sold at 4s each. It took another three years before the first 100 copies had been sold!

Even so, the house of Novello was beginning to take root and prosper. Already 'Music Sellers to their Royal Highnesses the Duke of Cambridge and the Duke of Gloucester', they were soon able to add the magic words 'By Appointment to Queen Adelaide' to their title pages, and by 1834 the business had expanded so greatly that the family, as we have seen, was obliged to move to larger premises at 69 Dean Street. Three years later they moved out altogether and 69 Dean Street became the publishing house proper. By 1845 a city office had been opened at 24 Poultry, at the sign of 'The Golden Crotchet', while Dean Street rejoiced in the sonorous and significant title: 'The London Sacred Music Warehouse'.

If any one year can be said to have been crucial in the establishment of the firm's success, it is probably 1836. Two important events took place. In March, J. Alfred Novello gave signal proof of his business enterprise and initiative by launching a magazine: *The Musical World*–a 'weekly record of Musical Science, Literature and Intelligence'. It was the first British magazine of its kind and its success was immediate. The mixture of news and gossip, reports on concerts and opera, both in London and the provinces, reviews of new music and short informative articles (the first issue contained 'A Sketch of the State of Music in England, from the Year 1778 up to the Present' by Samuel Wesley) proved to be just what the rising tide of middle-class music-lovers wanted. Published 'every Friday afternoon at five o'clock', at 3d for sixteen pages, it also proved to be a splendid vehicle, as doubtless J. Alfred intended, for the advertisement of Novello publications and the general dissemination of the firm's name.

The first editor, not altogether surprisingly, was Charles Cowden Clarke, and the magazine was to continue successfully, in other hands and under different proprietors, until 1891. In 1837, however, Alfred Novello decided to sell it. There seems to have been no special reason why he should have abandoned the venture so early in its career, and his decision to take over Mainzer's *Musical Times and Singing Circular* in 1844 rather suggests that he regretted having done so. But in *The Musical Times* he found a publication that was to exert an even greater influence.

The second important decision of 1836 was made clear in an announcement[5] that appeared in *The Musical World* on 25 March:

J. ALFRED NOVELLO

Begs to inform his friends, and those lovers of
Classical Music who favour him with their patronage,
that he has purchased the copyright for England of
"ST. PAUL,"
an oratorio
by
FELIX MENDELSSOHN BARTHOLDI

A piano score was to be available at 26s, with separate printed vocal and orchestral parts, all ready for delivery by 15 October, in good time for the first performance in England at the Liverpool Festival.

The overwhelming success of this work established the Novello catalogue, which by now included such items as Beethoven's Mass in C and Spohr's oratorio *The Last Judgment* (not to mention Sir Henry Bishop's 'Paradise Lost' cantata, *The Seventh Day*), as one of the most interesting and liberal on the London musical scene. For a fee of thirty guineas, J. Alfred Novello had lifted his firm into the front rank of British publishers. He now proceeded to consolidate his position.

His genius as a publisher lay in his ability to sense a social and artistic trend in its outset, and then back his instinct to the full. He recognized a need almost before it manifested itself, and promptly set about providing the material that would feed it.

At this point in the history of British music all the signs pointed to an enormous upsurge in choral singing. The English had always admired and encouraged choral singing, whether in the special field of the great cathedral service, or in the more public domain of Purcellian ode and Handelian oratorio. Moreover, a nation with so rich a tradition of poetry enjoyed an inevitable bias towards song in every form. Magnificent translations of the Bible and the sonorous language of the Book of Common Prayer brought further fuel to the movement. Singing, as long as it was not concerned with the artificialities of opera, was a fine and manly thing in British eyes–it was, so to speak, demonstrably healthy and democratic.

Nevertheless, large-scale choral singing, as exemplified in the eighteenth century by unique gatherings such as the Three Choirs Festival, though popular had been, in essence, the prerogative of the middle and upper classes because of the expense. But in the nineteenth century it was to become available virtually to everybody, regardless of rank and station. It was this trend that J. Alfred Novello recognized and was prepared to serve.

Not least among the portents was the gradual movement towards providing at least a basic education for all classes, and the hunger for self-improvement (through such bodies as the Mechanics' Institutes) shown by the workers themselves. But the privileged classes who were reluctantly preparing to acknowledge these needs, were also aware of the dangers they might unleash. It was here that music came in. The breast that swelled in song was, it was argued, less likely to be savage. Provided that the words carried a suitable message, singing could be an effective agent for social stability.

It would, however, be wrong to pretend that the great choral-singing movement was simply a plot to keep the lower classes in order. Most, if not all, of those who lent weight to the movement did so out of a genuine belief in its moral fitness. When Dr James Kay, secretary to the Committee of Council on Education, reported in the minutes of 1840–4 that singing was 'an important means of forming an industrious, brave, loyal, and religious people' he was stating an ideal, and not merely proposing a subtle antidote to Chartist unrest![6]

The movement took many forms. Among the most interesting were the efforts of Joseph Mainzer (1801–51) and John Hullah (1812–84) to teach music to the masses. During his early years in Germany,

Mainzer had published a teaching method that had been adopted in schools throughout Prussia. When political unrest forced him to leave his native land, he settled in Paris and in 1834 set up a series of astonishingly successful free classes in music and singing for workmen and artisans. A series of personal misfortunes prompted him to move to London, and in May 1841 he set up similar classes in Whitechapel, the Edgware Road and at the Elephant and Castle. To further his cause he began to issue, in August of the same year, a small information sheet which he called the *National Singing Circular*. This proved so popular that he was encouraged to expand it into a regular musical journal which, among other things, would contain in each number a piece of music suitable for choral singing. The new journal, *Mainzer's Musical Times and Singing Circular*, price 2d, made its first appearance on 15 July 1842, and its distribution was handled by J. Alfred Novello. When Mainzer moved to Edinburgh and Manchester, Novello's not only became the main agents for his music, but also took over the magazine, and in due course, on 1 June 1844, the first issue of *The Musical Times* appeared.

Hullah, on the other hand, was more concerned with the teaching of music in schools. On 1 February 1841 he opened, in London's Exeter Hall, a school for the instruction of schoolmasters in day and Sunday schools in the art of teaching singing in the Sol-fa method. Though bitterly attacked by his opponents (he used the rather limited 'fixed doh' method proposed by Guillaume Wilhem in France in the 1820s), his scheme was enormously successful and the classes were attended not only by teachers but also by the general public.

Among those who visited Hullah's classes was John Curwen (1816–80), a young teacher who had been investigating a method of sol-fa teaching which Miss Sarah Glover (1786–1867) was using with great success in Norwich. This method, which hinged upon a 'movable doh', he adapted into the highly practical Tonic Sol-fa system which later enabled thousands of amateur singers to participate in choral singing without having to undergo the lengthy and rather specialized process of learning standard musical notation.

Of equal importance to the development of singing in schools and among the working classes, was the resurgence of choir music in churches other than cathedrals and college chapels. The re-establishment of the choral service, after the two centuries of neglect that followed the English Reformation, was an important aspect of the so-called Oxford Movement which sought to revitalize and purify the

manner of worship in Victorian England. Probably the most outstanding example of this new attitude was to be found at Margaret
Chapel in London's Marylebone during the incumbency of the Revd
Frederick Oakley, beginning in 1839. Little by little, in the teeth of
outraged cries of 'Popery!', the great choral revival took root, and
soon the surpliced choir of men and boys became an accepted feature
even of parochial church worship.

Although working from an opposite point of view, the position of
music in the Methodist and Evangelical churches was almost equally
important in spreading a love of singing through all classes. Here it
was the heartfelt singing of sturdy hymns by the entire congregation
that mattered—complex choral polyphony, as executed by trained
choirs, was anathema in their acts of worship. The point at issue,
however, was that the congregations sang, and sang lustily. And if
they could not abide anthems, they extended no such scruples to the
singing of oratorios and concerts of sacred music, even in consecrated
buildings.

A further aspect of the changing climate of the times is described in
the leading article of the first issue of *The Musical Times*, published
under the title, *The Amateurs of London*. It was, presumably, written by
the first editor, J. Alfred Novello himself:

It is satisfactory to those who desire and have laboured for the
general diffusion of a taste for music amongst all classes of the
community, to observe the sure results of what has been doing
for the last few years.

Some twenty years since, the execution of concerted and
choral music in private was almost unknown; indeed it then
required more than ordinary industry to organise such a performance. The libraries of the few, who possessed classical
works then only in MS had to be visited, much diligence used in
multiplying sufficiently the copies, and then the small number of
performers who could be got together, although 'willing', were
far from 'able to take a part.' Some zealous individuals, about the
time mentioned, formed themselves into a society called the
'Classical Harmonists,' and such was the existing scarcity of able
amateurs, that for several years their limited number of some
twenty members, 'willing and able to take a part,' remained
incomplete.

This society was the parent of many other associations, having for their object the performance of somewhat similar music; and such was the influence of this constant private performance of the highest classical works, and the production of good printed copies, on the taste and practical ability of the amateurs of London, that we find in 1834 that there was designed and effectively carried into execution, the Amateur Festival–a meeting which was highly creditable to all engaged, and was very beneficial to the excellent charity to which the surplus funds were dedicated. The taste for this rational and delightful manner of passing the evening has so much increased since 1834 that the many important societies existing in London are more in number than the individual members required for the formation of the parent society, besides the numerous friendly meetings where the young people of neighbouring families join for the execution of concerted music.[7]

It seems clear, then, that in the 1840s everything in English musical life was conspiring to one end: an enormous increase in music-making of every kind, and in particular of its most democratic aspect–choral singing. The publisher who sensed what was in the air would undoubtedly make a killing. And it is equally clear, as a further article in that first *Musical Times* proves, that J. Alfred Novello knew that the moment was to hand:

A very important contribution to the cause of good music has been made by the publication of several numbers of a series of 'Cheap Classics.' They are printed in vocal score with a separate accompaniment for the organ or pianoforte; great pains having been taken with the engraving and printing, so that they are emphatically 'cheap' both in quantity and quality. For instance, Spohr's great oratorio of 'The Last Judgment' is complete for 7s 6d; Mozart's Masses at 2s 6d and 3s 6d each; and Haydn's Masses from 4s to 6s.

It is probable that this experiment to give the public music at a cheaper rate than usual, will be attended with better success than has hithertoo been the case; because former reprints have usually consisted of non-copyright works already to be found in a great variety of shapes. But the present series consists of standard and much-sought-after works, only previously to be obtained at a high price.

The last month has also produced the concluding numbers of Boyce's collection of Cathedral Music printed in separate Vocal Parts. Choral Societies can now perform some of the services produced by the great English Cathedral writers, which previously to the present publication were sealed books. It will doubtless be one means of that great improvement so much to be desired, in the Cathedral and Church Service, as a very extensive choir can be supplied with sufficient copies at a trifling cost.

It is intended that the valuable collection of cathedral music made by Dr Arnold be immediately published in the same manner in separate vocal parts.[8]

What he may also have begun to appreciate was that in 1841 he had taken under his wing a young man in whom he could trust the future development of the firm which was now so manifestly flourishing.

CHAPTER FIVE

HENRY LITTLETON

In 1841 Henry Littleton was eighteen years old. He had been born in London in 1823, and the story of his early life has the authentic ring of Victorian rags-to-riches romance. It seems that at fourteen he was desperately looking for employment when he met, quite by chance in St Paul's churchyard, another boy of the same age who told him that his own firm, the music publisher George & Manby at 85 Fleet Street, was looking for an office boy. Within a few minutes Henry Littleton had secured the vacant post and his career in music had begun. A chance meeting with a different boy, working in a different trade, might have produced equally striking results, for the matter of 'vocation' simply did not arise: Henry Littleton was a boy in poor circumstances in need of work and determined to succeed at whatever fate had in store for him.

From George & Manby he moved to another house in the same line of business (Monro & May, 11 Holborn Bars) and then, in 1841, to Novello's as a 'collector'. Even this progression argues an early astuteness, for neither George & Manby nor Monro & May continued to operate after 1848 (though May survived, on his own, until 1862).

The collector's duty was to make a daily round of all the London publishers, gathering in those items that his own firm's customers had ordered but which were not necessarily held in stock. This obliging and civilized custom lingered on until the middle of the present century. Nowadays the customer fends for himself. Foot-wearing though the job may have been, it had one aspect from which an incipient tycoon might profit: the intimate knowledge of what each rival firm was publishing, and how well individual types of music were selling.

Such was Henry Littleton's energy and ability that, within a very few years, he had risen to a position of trust in Alfred Novello's eyes. It seems probable that there was a certain bond of reserved affection between them–Alfred seeing, perhaps, in Henry Littleton the son he never had. A letter written from Liverpool on 10 August 1844 has, for all its period formality, a touching warmth:

> Dear Sir,
>   It gives me great pleasure to hear from Mr [Cowden] Clarke of your continued attention to your duties in Dean Street, not only from the comfort and confidence it gives me personally during my absence, but also as it assures me that the good opinion I had formed of you has not been mis-placed, and is a good promise of your future welfare.
>   This 12th of Aug (the day on which you will receive this) is my birthday, and I have therefore chosen it as a pleasant opportunity to send you the enclosed five pounds of which I request your acceptance, as a mark of my approbation. I hope that you will by perseverance in the same conduct make yourself a useful member of society, and earn yourself the satisfaction of meriting my future confidence.
>   I remain,
>   with sincere good wishes for your advancement,
>   Yours faithfully,
>   J. Alfred Novello[1]

In the 1840s Alfred Novello had every reason to be grateful to a loyal and energetic member of the staff, for he had entered upon the most ambitious, exciting and undoubtedly nerve-wracking period of his business career. The association with Mendelssohn, sealed by the purchase of the *St Paul* copyright in 1836, had deepened over the years to their mutual advantage. A third book of *Songs without Words* had been purchased in September 1837, together with Three Preludes and Fugues for organ and three short choral pieces for female voices (all for £35), and in the following month forty guineas secured the copyright on the Piano Concerto in D minor, in time for the Birmingham Festival where Mendelssohn was to play it. The *42nd Psalm* copyright was purchased in 1838 for fifteen guineas, and that of the *Hymn of Praise* for just twenty-five guineas in 1840.

Nor were other composers neglected. In 1842 Novello's brought out the first English edition of Rossini's *Stabat Mater*, and in 1846 a new edition, with accompaniments arranged by Vincent Novello, of Beethoven's *Missa Solemnis* in preparation for the famous Philharmonic Society performance under Sir Michael Costa which finally revealed to English audiences that the work was, after all, both practical and a masterpiece.

And then, in July 1846, there appeared a most important advertisement,[2] announcing with a wealth of exclamation marks:

"The cheapest Musical Publication ever offered to the public,
in respect both to quality and quantity!!!"

———

"Handel's Sacred Oratorio
'THE MESSIAH'
in Vocal Score
With separate accompaniment for the Organ or
Pianoforte
Arranged by
VINCENT NOVELLO."

The whole work was to be completed in twelve monthly numbers, price 6d each, and publication would commence on 1 August 1846.

Alfred Novello's excited superlatives are excusable. At one courageous stroke he had brought a prime example of great music within the budgets of ordinary people. Even if you could not afford the complete bound copy at 6s 6d, you could buy each part month by month and sew them together yourself, perhaps using one of the specially designed 'Parchment Cloth Cases' also available at the same price. If novels could appear successfully in monthly instalments, why not music? What was good for Dickens's publishers might equally well be good for a Novello! And if the excitement of wondering what might 'happen next month' was not built into a work as popular as the *Messiah*, later works issued in the same manner were almost bound to contain the surprise of unfamiliarity.

The serialized *Messiah* proved a great success, and Haydn's *Creation* was promptly published in the same format (nine 6d numbers sufficed). Then *Judas Maccabaeus*, and *Jeptha* and so on—Vincent Novello himself preparing and editing no fewer than eighteen such large-scale works. The more the market was fed, the greater the demand. The greater the demand, the more the price could be brought down. Accordingly, in January 1849, Alfred Novello astounded the music publishing world by cutting his prices in half. He set out the equation in a neat pamphlet[3] that he published on New Year's day. The argument ran thus:

The cost of copyright, or payment to the Author :   10. 10. 0d
The cost of plates, engraving, etc: 10. 0. 0d
The cost of printing and paper for 200 copies :   15. 0. 0d

_____

£35. 10. 0d

The expense divided amongst 200 purchasers,
is 3s. 6d. each.

But suppose a larger number of purchasers:
The cost to the Author and for engraving,
   etc as before :   20. 10. 0d
The cost of printing and paper for 2,000 copies,
   same rate as before :   150. 0. 0d

_____

£170. 10. 0d

Expense divided amongst 2,000 purchasers, is about
1s. 9d. each.

Assuming it was a correct estimation of the market's needs, the argument was irrefutable.

By 1849, however, Alfred Novello had become his own printer, taking on additional premises at Dean's Yard, 21 Dean Street, for the purpose. Though forced upon him by circumstances, the step was very much in accord with the essentially practical cast of his mind, for, as we shall see in later chapters, it was to technical matters that he always turned for pleasure and relaxation. The moment of decision came in 1847 when Mr Joseph Surman, a music publisher with whom Alfred Novello had considerable dealings, was removed from his position as conductor of the Sacred Harmonic Society. Not altogether surprisingly, he took the vocal scores and orchestral parts of his own publications with him and refused to let the society purchase new sets. Alfred Novello, who had acted as agent for many of Surman's publications, now found himself unable to supply his customers. Typically, he saw in this set-back a worthy challenge and promptly announced:

> I have taken immediate steps to repair this temporary inconvenience by engraving the whole of the parts, which I have been induced to advertise in my catalogue, and considerable progress is already made with them; but as it is unavoidably a work requiring time, my friends, I hope, will have a little patience with me. I will, however, use all diligence, and I can promise them that they shall not long be deprived of the power of purchasing parts, even if Mr Surman should not awaken to a sense of what he owes to the public who have hithertoo supported him. The present unexpected course of Mr Surman is not altogether without its public advantage, for I am in a manner forced to undertake the printing of these parts, which I should not otherwise have done and I am thereby enabled to introduce all those improvements which have been so much required.[4]

Any chagrin Mr Surman may have felt must have been doubly underlined by the note of smugness that Mr Novello could not quite stifle.

In becoming his own printer, however, Alfred Novello had first to face the problems arising out of certain trade union rules for compositors governing the setting up of letter-type in combination with music-type. Having decided that he wished to take advantage of the new and improved music founts which Messrs William Clowes had cut, and which could endure the pulling of many more impressions than an engraved plate, he found that the cost of setting up words with music was nearly double the cost of setting up the same measure of words alone. He thereupon promptly engaged non-union men and went ahead on his own terms. Though by present-day standards it was a buccaneering attitude—one wonders if Karl Marx, scribbling away at *Das Kapital* in his miserable lodgings at 26 Dean Street ever got to hear about it!—it was not unusual in the nineteenth century. Significantly, within three years the union relaxed its rules, having realized that they were indeed unnecessarily restrictive.

It was at this point that Alfred Novello decided to adopt the now common 'royal octavo' size for his publications, as a cheaper alternative to the more usual 'folio' editions.

The idea of an 'octavo edition' had its origin in the size selected for

The Musical Times. Its policy, inherited from Mainzer, of including a piece of sacred or secular music in each issue had proved that the size itself was perfectly practicable. The new type-face was sharp and clear and admirably suited to more extended works. The size of the printed words was in easy relationship with the size of the printed notes and both were easy to read at the normal distance. The sheer physical weight of a vocal score was considerably reduced, and the whole thing made easier to handle as a result. Indeed, it was now possible to balance a complete vocal score on the palm of one hand, should the need arise. Choirs were delighted: sales went up, prices went down, and the octavo edition has been a standard size of vocal score ever since.

If Alfred Novello's decision to use music-type in preference to engraved plates seems strange, he had excellent reasons which he made clear in a pamphlet he published in 1847. After illustrating the merits of the new founts of music (in four different sizes), which he had had specially cut and cast by Mr Palmer of the Soho Type Foundry, he goes on to explain 'The Economics of Musick Printing' in the following terms:

> The probable number of copies to be sold, must decide whether it be more advisable to produce the work on Engraved Pewter Plates, or by Moveable Musick Types. The cost of producing a page of musick on a Pewter Plate is comparatively small; and there is the further advantage of being able to print *fifty* copies only from it as economically as any number of hundreds, thereby saving the accumulation of useless stock, and the loss of interest on the cost of the paper–great advantages in a work of slow or doubtful sale, or the demand for which is likely to be limited. The disadvantages of this mode are, the early wearing out of the plates (from 1300 to 2000 impressions, according to the goodness of the workmanship), and also the comparatively high cost of the printing.
>
> The page produced by Musick Types must be costly, because the types are expensive to purchase, and require considerable time and skill to compose them into the required page; but for any work of which a large number of impressions is wanted, they offer many advantages. By the process of Stereotyping,[5] a very large number of pages can be successively produced from a fount of type, and still leave the type at liberty to compose fresh pages.

Moveable Musick Types are particularly well adapted for the production of books on the science of musick, or where the musical examples are subordinate to the descriptions or comments which form the main part of the work. The economy of printing from these Types arises from the shorter time required to ink the projecting surfaces, and in the power to print several pages by the same operation: with care, the number of impressions which one Stereo-plate will yield may be said to be without limit. Of the disadvantages formerly existing against Musick Types, an important one has been removed by the increased varieties of characters; and any musick, however complicated, can now be produced with them. The great object with the publisher of a work from Moveable Type being to sell a *very large number* of copies, he usually marks the price of his work proportionally low to increase the sale.

There are several other considerations which it is impossible to enter into fully in this short sketch; but in order to decide which method offers most advantages, due consideration must be had to the nature of the work to be printed. It may be shortly stated, that for works of which *hundreds* only are expected to be required, Plates are the better method; but where *thousands* are required, the Moveable Types are decidedly preferable.[6]

Having arranged his printing house to his liking, Alfred Novello now turned his attention to the three government 'taxes on knowledge' which so enraged the progressive thinkers of the day: the excise duty (3d on each lb of paper), the stamp duty (1d on each sheet of newspaper) and the advertisement tax (1s 6d on each entry). In the clamour for the repeal of each of these repressive taxes he played a prominent and vociferous part.

As a music publisher he found he was peculiarly liable to bureaucratic lunacies. The fact that he published works in monthly numbers, each with a paper wrapper to keep them clean, meant that he became liable for advertisement tax because each wrapper bore a date and made reference to the firm's other recent publications. When he wanted to send *The Musical Times* through the post he found himself subject to the Newspaper Act, which not only required every proprietor to give security for the payment of advertisement duty, but also to enter into recognizances of £1200 that he would not insert a libel into the publication, 'an offence which', he sardonically pointed out, 'the nature of the work renders scarcely possible'.[7] As for the excise duty on paper, that burden spoke for itself.

Fighting side by side with 'The Apostle of Free Trade', Richard Cobden, and acting as treasurer of the Repeal Fund, Alfred Novello petitioned the House of Commons (8 April 1850) for the removal of the offensive taxes. Something of the nonsense he had to contend with can be seen in an editorial announcement printed in *The Musical Times* for April 1855:

> During the course of the sixth volume we have been threatened with a Government prosecution, because the Musical Times was said to be a *Newspaper*, and therefore ought not to be printed except upon stamped paper. The periodical has also been threatened to be sent to the Dead Letter Office by another department of the same Government, unless folded in a particular manner, because it was said to be *not strictly a Newspaper*.[8]

But by that time the advertisement duty had been abandoned (1853), and the 'red stain of bondage', the newspaper stamp, was about to be repealed. The duty on paper, however, remained until 1861.

In the meantime, the Novello catalogue grew and grew, and its range increased. Customers of almost every creed and inclination could now find something in it to their taste, whether music of the Roman Rite, which had first established the firm, or anthems, chants and services for the Anglican Church. Even dissenters could find comfort in the volume of *Surrey Chapel Music*, published in 1845 in sixteen instalments and backed by a list of 250 subscribers. There were individual songs, glees and madrigals; organ music (much of it edited by the indefatigable Vincent Novello); examples of Gregorian Chant, including J. Alfred Novello's own *Concise Explanation of the Gregorian Note* (1848); cantatas and oratorios; books of psalmody; and even a select list of miscellaneous instrumental pieces ('flute music, a speciality'). The 1847 catalogue runs to 130 pages–a testimony to the remarkable strides J. Alfred Novello had made in the first seventeen years of his career as a music publisher.

CHAPTER SIX

THE ROAD TO CHEAP MUSIC

If fellow publishers found themselves aghast at the implications of Alfred Novello's innovations, the general public entertained few doubts. An article published in a *Morning Herald* of the period (1849) neatly sums up the average music-lover's reaction:

> These works are issued at a price that literally places them within the reach of the million. The size (royal octavo) scarcely exceeds that of many operatic librettos, and hence the value of the publications as companions to the concert-room; while the exquisite beauty of the typography and the tasteful illumination of the binding give them a drawing-room character, which will also be duly prized and applauded. Although the type is small, it is wonderfully distinct, and in this respect is greatly superior to the printing by metal plates, with which modern ingenuity has made us familiar; but, above all, the oratorios emanate from the press under the control and supervision of Mr Vincent Novello, whose name ensures the fidelity of the text, and the certainty that the responsibilities of editorship are vigilantly and critically discharged. The success of the enterprise has, we believe, been unbounded; and we have been informed that some 20,000 copies of 'The Messiah' alone have already been sold.[1]

Having created a market for choral music of all kinds, Alfred Novello was quick to find new ways of feeding it. In March 1850 he issued a prospectus for a 'Novello Part-Song Book', to be edited by Edwin George Monk and printed in quarto vocal score at 12s, with separate octavo vocal parts at 1s 6d each. The sum of £100 was to be expended each year in prizes of eight guineas for the best part-song in four voices, the character of the music being required to be 'vigorous and terse, attractive yet solid'.[2] The details of the prospectus tell us much about the climate of the period:

In the present day a knowledge and love of Music are increasing so much amongst us, that England appears to be returning to her condition nearly three centuries since, when every social meeting was cheered by the practised skill of its members, and when a gentleman was held to be but imperfectly educated who could not take his part 'at sight' in a madrigal.

The enormous demand for vocal music thus created, and which is every day increasing, has hithertoo been met, almost exclusively, by the exhumation of the madrigals which delighted our forefathers, and by the reproduction of the glees of a more recent age. Beautiful as many of these compositions are, and becoming as it may be for us affectionately to use such stores of harmony, yet it is believed that *new* vocal music, written in a style at once masculine and correct, will be welcomed, as well as by those concerned in the education of youth, as by the domestic circle, and the choral society.

In the present Work it is proposed to publish original compositions of this character; in supplying which, the Editor will be assisted by several able and accepted writers, who have kindly offered him their valuable co-operation.

There is also a class of music sung with excellent effect in Germany, which is not represented by either the madrigals, glees, or ballads now in use amongst ourselves—namely, bold choral melodies of so marked and emphatic a character, as to require little previous study in the singers. These, too, linked as they are with spirit-stirring words, can scarcely fail to ensure an animated and simultaneous execution. It is intended to select some of the most striking of these German choruses and part-songs, for insertion in the present Collection; for which purpose they will carefully be fitted with appropriate English words, either original or otherwise.

But it has a further object. The words of too many old English madrigals and part-songs betray a painful want of refinement; and, when graver objections than this do not lie against them, are often intolerable from their unmeaning frivolity. Hence it is thought that many persons might gladly avail themselves of a Collection of concerted pieces, the words of which should be, not only inoffensive, but calculated to encourage a vigorous and cheerful tone of mind, equally removed from coarseness and sentimentality...[3]

The prizes, however, did not inspire many hitherto unknown geniuses, and the firm was acutely embarrassed when one composer, the young Walter Macfarren, carried off the first three awards. Rather than compromise the scheme in its very infancy, they came to an understanding whereby Miss Elizabeth Stirling was allowed to take the second of the prizes, but were driven to ask him to refrain altogether from competing when it was discovered that he had won the third round. After seven prizes had been awarded the competition was abandoned, but the policy of publishing a consistent stream of part-songs continued and proved a vital stimulus to young British composers. Names such as George Alexander Macfarren, Julius Benedict, John Liptrot Hatton, Joseph Barnby, Arthur Sullivan, Henry Hiles and Henry Leslie begin to appear, and many of the pieces they produced for this market (Macfarren's *Seven Shakespeare Songs*, for example) are of a very high order.

At first, however, it seems that the public did not respond wholeheartedly, so in October 1855 Alfred Novello issued a plaintive appeal 'To Choral, Vocal, and Glee Societies':

It is a curious part of my long experience to find that after twenty-five years I feel more and more doubtful in deciding what will suit popular taste. The most signal instance of this is, I think, presented by the book I printed a short time since, called Novello's PART-SONG BOOK; a work which has not yet had the sale and success which I expected, and which it deserves, from the expense, labour, and attention bestowed on its production.[4]

After detailing the book's many virtues ('The subjects of the Part-Songs are especially addressed to National and Patriotic feelings...') he continues:

Now what I have to ask is, that my good friends in the Societies to whom this is addressed will consider what I have left undone,– what they would advise me to do,–or what change (if any) they would propose in the PART-SONG BOOK, to make so valuable a collection of carefully selected new part-songs a useful contribution to the vocal societies of the day.[5]

Evidently the public was revived, for a second series was begun shortly after, which eventually went on to embrace more than seven hundred numbers by the end of the century.

At the same time as stimulating new music, Alfred Novello was careful to continue exploring the old. The Novello 'Glee-Hive'–a collection of the most popular glees and madrigals–was begun in 1850. We learn from *The Musical Times* of December 1850 that a new piece will be 'ready each week, and will vary in price according to the length, at the rate of one half-penny per page'.[6] Moreover, for the convenience of those who might purchase the collection in monthly instalments, 'they will be done up in a neat wrapper in time for the Magazines'.[7]

The first numbers included pieces by R. J. S. Stevens, John Benet, Samuel Webbe, John Stafford Smith, Reginald Spofforth, Luca Marenzio, the Earl of Mornington and Orlando di Lasso–as catholic a spread as anyone could wish. On completion of the first volume (containing twenty-six numbers) Alfred Novello permitted himself a delightfully fanciful preface, complete with a quotation from the Bard (by courtesy, doubtless, of the Cowden Clarkes):

> Like the bee, tolling from every flower
> The virtuous sweets;
> Our thighs pack'd with wax, our mouths with honey,
> We bring it to the Hive.
> > *Shakespeare*

Our first Hive is full: like the humane bee-hive of modern invention it enables us to bind up our sweets, and send them forth to the musical honey-lover, without impairing our power of collecting fresh stores for future gratification. The contents of our first Glee Hive offers a fair specimen of what we are enabled to gather from the School of Music which Englishmen have made so completely their own; and in the profusion of fair flowers which exist in the *English Glee garden*, we shall find ample material to fill many a goodly hive.

We trust to proceed in our future labours with the regularity and industry of our insect model; punctually producing our weekly Glee, or Madrigal; and, with the Bee's discrimination, bringing to our Hive only the sweetness of Glee-honey, or the sterling value of Madrigal-wax.[8]

A similar preface to the second volume (July 1851) harks back, perhaps unconsciously, to childhood days and the four leather-bound manuscript books of Vincent Novello's *Music for the Open Air*: 'We trust our two completed volumes will be found valued companions at the summer ramble or pic-nic, when the well-remembered favourites of last winter's rehearsals shall serve to awaken the echoes in some shady resting place'.[9] Not everything associated with these and similar publications was, however, quite so idyllic. Such was the demand for new music that Alfred Novello found himself having to take legal action to defend his copyrights:

It has come to the knowledge of the Proprietors of *Novello's Part-Song Book*, that their copyrights have been multiplied by musical societies and others who have made manuscript and, sometimes, printed copies for the use of their singers, instead of using the copyright editions. Legal steps have been taken to defend their rights against such transgressors as have yet been discovered, and the proceedings will be published when they have reached a more advanced stage; but, in the meantime, the present CAUTION is given to deter others from committing similar piracies.[10]

The particular transgressor in this instance was Mr Sudlow, the conductor of the Liverpool Philharmonic Society. The case came to the Court of Common Pleas in 1852, appropriately enough before, amongst others, Sir Edward Vaughan Williams, grandfather of the composer. Sudlow was shown to have purchased a copy of Julius Benedict's part-song *The Wreath*, to have had 250 lithographic impressions taken and to have distributed them 'gratuitously' to the members of his choir. His defence lay, somewhat ingenuously, in his benevolence in not actually charging for the copies, or hiring them out. The usual legal procedures were gone through with due solemnity (a more than commonly fatuous counsel for the defence at one point suggesting that 'the honour and glory of authorship is its sufficient award'), but, in the end, the Lord Chief Justice (Sir John Jervis) found for the plaintiff.

A similar verdict had been reached in the previous year when action had been taken against the publisher of a periodical called *The Pianista*, who had pirated the first book of Mendelssohn's *Songs without Words* whose British copyright Novello's had finally bought outright in September 1837.

There was also the even trickier business of reassuring the timorous music-seller. By cutting his prices in half in 1849, J. Alfred Novello caused the proprietors of certain shops to protest that he was reducing their share of the profits. Some, it seems, took action, and in December 1851 *The Musical Times* carried the following warning:

> Certain Music-sellers, in town and country, appear to think that this concession to the public interferes with their interests, not perceiving that an increased consumption more than makes up to them for the change; and they interfere in various ways to deprive the public of the benefit, by stating 'Novello's Editions are out of print,' or trying to sell other copies marked at a higher price, and sometimes even by altering the Prices printed on my publications.
>
> THE PUBLIC FOR THEIR OWN PROTECTION
> Should therefore:–
> 1st.– Insist on having 'Novello's Editions,' which are always in print, and can be obtained by every respectable Music-seller or Bookseller in town or country.
> 2nd.– Compare the price they pay with the Catalogue prices.
> 3rd.– If other methods fail, address their orders direct to The Public's Obedient Servant, J. Alfred Novello.[11]

Though the success of his publications lay mainly in their quality and good value, Alfred's personal attention to their promotion also played its part. Taking advantage of the new railways, in which he was already an eager investor, he travelled up and down the country, meeting the choral societies that were popping up everywhere, listening to and encouraging their efforts, and giving freely of his advice. Small wonder, then, that when performances took place it was with the aid of the new Novello scores—a fact on which he was quick to capitalize in his carefully worded advertisements:

> As the winter advances, and the longer darkness of the evenings
> gives more time for in-door amusements before it is bed-time,
> MUSIC (which has been disregarded during summer) resumes
> her sway. Holiday-making at the sea-side, or by excursion trains,
> has come to an end, and the scattered members of practising
> Vocal and Orchestral Societies re-organise their meetings with
> fresh appetite from the recess. The natural sequence is to ask what
> has Mr Alfred Novello been providing for us?[12]

The answer on this occasion (November 1853) included oratorios by the Chevalier Neukomm, Handel's *Deborah*, and Henry Hugo Pierson's *Jerusalem*—in addition to *The Deliverance of Israel from Babylon*, and *Isaiah*, both by Mr Jackson, of Masham. And for choral societies with little money to spend, all the choruses from the major oratorios could now be obtained individually at prices ranging from 1½d to 6d. Ferdinand Hiller's 125th Psalm, 'produced at Dusseldorf last May', is not included because, we are told, the 'Parts are still to be engraved'.[13]

Having attended to the needs of his fellow-countrymen, J. Alfred Novello had also begun to explore the possibilities of a North American market. There is some evidence to suggest that an agency agreement was reached with Firth Hall and Pound, 239 Broadway, New York, in about 1847. Advertisements in *The Musical Times* for December 1851 refer to agents in Boston (G. P. Reed) and New York (W. Hall and sons). The change argues a degree of difficulty in setting up a satisfactory outlet, and the problem seems to have continued, for in the summer of 1852 Novello's sent out a trusted assistant to run a shop of their own at 389 Broadway, New York. An advertisement in *The Musical Times* for December 1852 carries an invigorating description of the benefits they hoped to confer on the New Yorkers:

> Few are aware how readily the means of an efficient performance
> of these classical, four-voice works can be provided by the
> meeting of three or four families—one lady or gentleman to
> preside at the Piano, and the rest to take their respective Soprano,
> Alto, Tenor, and Bass parts; studying their music previously to
> the meeting, which in most places can conveniently take place
> once a week, alternately, perhaps, at the houses of each family.

One source of success in England has been the disconnecting of MUSIC (as here proposed) from its oppressors–LATE HOURS, OSTENTATIOUS EXPENSE, and mere PARTY-GIVING: freed in this manner, some of the best music in England is performed by, say, six families meeting in succession at their parents' houses, all idle, or uninterested listeners being excluded; the hour of meeting, seven o'clock; music for two hours; tea, and its strict concomitants, at nine; and then an hour of lighter music enables each to depart for home at half-past ten. An evening so spent leaves nothing to regret the next day...[14]

The music, we are told, would be available 'for Ready Money at the same prices as in Britain, 25 cents to the shilling sterling'.[15]

From the very beginning of his publishing career, J. Alfred Novello had kept a watchful eye open for sales of plates and copyrights when rival publishers ceased to trade. For example, in 1836 he acquired certain plates of Messrs Paine & Hopkins, and in 1849 a selection of those belonging to Coventry & Hollier, his neighbour at 71 Dean Street. A much greater haul came in 1851 when Charles Coventry abandoned the attempt to continue as a publisher on his own. Novello's purchased 4780 plates of mainly sacred music, together with some 1427 plates of the newly engraved edition of Mozart's pianoforte works, edited by Cipriani Potter, principal of the Royal Academy of Music. These were later published in nine volumes at a cost of seven guineas (Coventry had charged sixteen!). They could also be purchased fortnightly in parts at 4s 6d each. As a further innovation, a thematic catalogue was prepared, the first of its kind to be published in this country.

Further evidence of the firm's enterprise is to be found in 1852 with the announcement of 'The Library for the Diffusion of Musical Knowledge'. The first publication consisted of a translation, by George Macirone, of Dr Adolph Marx's *Allgemeine Musiklehre* (under the title *General Musical Instruction*) in three volumes. It was followed by Cherubini's *Treatise on Counterpoint*, translated from the French by Mary Cowden Clarke, Charles-Simon Catel's *Treatise on Harmony* (translated by the same hand) and Albrechtsberger's *Collected Writings on Thorough-Bass, Harmony, and Composition, for Self-Instruction*, translated by Sabilla Novello, with music examples 'revised' by Vincent Novello. Sabilla also provided a translation of the so-called Mozart *Succinct Thorough-Bass School*, and wrote a very popular book of her own, *Voice and Vocal Art*. Later additions to the series include Dr Crotch's *Elements of Musical Composition* and, most daring of all, Mary Cowden Clarke's translation of Hector Berlioz's *Treatise on Modern Instrumentation and Orchestration*—for which he wrote, for a fee of £40, an entirely new chapter on the duties of the conductor.

Add to this galaxy of musical instruction a splendid two-volume edition of Sir John Hawkins's *General History of the Science and Practice of Music*, published in November 1852 at 35s, with a supplementary volume of portraits at 16s, and Thomas Goodban's 'Pack of Fifty-two Music Cards, with a Book of Instructions for playing a variety of Instructive and Entertaining Games on the rudiments and funda-mental principles of the science of Music: written, invented, and designed for the purpose of combining instruction with amusement' (price 5s), and it can be seen that Novello's aimed to please at every level.

It is also clear that the firm was delighted with its own progress and anxious that the world should hear about it. The display stand which J. Alfred Novello designed in 1854 for the Crystal Palace (newly erected at Sydenham) is a masterly example of Victorian ebullience, ingenuity, and doubtful taste. According to Richard Cobden it was one of the talking points of the entire exhibition—the other being Clara Novello's voice ('the throat of a bird, the voice of an angel, and the enthusiasm of a patriot' declared *The Musical World*), which rose to a thrilling high B flat in the National Anthem. ('Clara Novello's fine voice sounded so well in that large space', the Queen confided to her diary.)[16]

As seen in earlier chapters, however, this was also a period when the close domestic circle enjoyed and exploited by the Novellos was beginning to break up. In 1848 Mrs Novello retired to Nice, where she was joined by Vincent in the following year. She died in 1854, and two years later, in October 1856, J. Alfred Novello announced his own retirement. Though he had reason enough to give up work—he had devoted twenty-six years to building up the firm, and now had all the money he needed—it seems more than likely that his mother's death set him free. He had done what she wanted. Now he would withdraw and follow the engineering schemes that were so close to his heart. More-over, he knew that in Henry Littleton he had someone to whom he could hand over the business in complete confidence.

Virtually the entire Novello clan went to live at the Villa Quaglia: Vincent, Alfred, Sabilla, and Charles and Mary Cowden Clarke. Near them, for at least a part of every year, were the Gigliuccis and their four children ('the most adorable human cherubs I ever beheld', declared Mary Cowden Clarke).[17] And here they settled to a routine of family conviviality not unlike the days of their Oxford Street childhood. Distinguished visitors came from all over the world, some to talk about Shakespeare and Chaucer with the Cowden Clarkes, others to talk about music with Vincent and Alfred. There were parties, and frequent amateur theatricals. It was all very pleasant.

But not everything was well in Nice itself. As part of the Kingdom of Sardinia it had become involved in Napoleon III's schemes to liberate northern Italy from Austria. The battles of Magenta and Solferino brought matters to a head in March 1860. The Novellos, led by Mary Cowden Clarke, were indignant:

> What with utter repugnance to the thought of being handed over to France, to live under the rule of an arch-liar, to be under French government, and what with the nausea of hearing the topic constantly and angrily discussed, I feel thoroughly worn out with the subject. The Count, I feel assured, will never submit to live under French domination, therefore the Gigliuccis will certainly remove, should Nice no longer be Italian; Sabilla is a red-hot Italy-woman, and Alfred has adopted the partisanship.[18]

The deciding factor came when it was suddenly announced that the Villa Quaglia, which they were renting, was to be sold. Fortunately Alfred and Sabilla had already set their hearts on a house in Genoa. The Cowden Clarkes approved and the purchase went ahead. Alfred and Sabilla took possession in April 1861 and set about making it habitable. For the time being Mary, Charles and Vincent remained in Nice.

Vincent Novello was destined never to move to the new house. On 9 August, a month or so before his eightieth birthday, he died, and the last link with the old life was broken.

Before the year was out, on 8 October 1861, Alfred Novello had entered into a formal partnership with Henry Littleton with an agreement to sell him the business, on the understanding that the family's name would never be dropped.

The terms of this agreement were remarkable. Henry Littleton had prospered with the firm, but had almost no capital. It is true he owned the plates and copyright in Michael Balfe's arrangement of Tom Moore's *Irish Melodies*, and had set up a separate business as music printer from engraved plates at 24 Cornwall Road, Lambeth. But these were not assets of any significance. There was only one way in which he could buy the firm—and it was, presumably, owing to Alfred Novello's generosity that the ingenious solution was found.

The partnership agreement was calculated on a ten-year basis, during which time Alfred Novello was to draw out £2500 every six months, while Henry Littleton made do with £200. Surplus profits above £500 could be paid in advance to Alfred Novello if Henry Littleton so wished. At the end of ten years, when Alfred Novello had drawn a total of £50,000, the firm would be Henry Littleton's property. The agreement could be terminated if the balance on each year's profits was not sufficient to meet the annual sum required by Alfred Novello.

It meant, of course, that Henry Littleton, living modestly on £400 a year, must make the firm yield a clear annual profit of at least £5500—more, if he was to steer the business into a confident future. But this is precisely what he did. Such was his success that the £50,000 was paid off in five years, and on 17 September 1866 he became the sole proprietor of Novello & Company.

Alfred Novello, however, could afford to be generous. Over the years he had made shrewd investments. A will, dated May 1858, shows him to have been in possession of shares in railway stock (the London and North Western Railway, the Great Western, the Worcester and Hereford, and the Chester and Holyhead) to the tune of £5535. Other members of the family held similar amounts, 'The Funds' being managed by Alfred. He, and they, also held Scandinavian bonds of some consequence, shares in the Crystal Palace Company, a balance of £2500 in the Bank of London, and, most important of all, the patent rights for Sardinia of the new Bessemer Iron Process, with a half share in the same for Sweden. Add to this various rents from property in Croydon, Hemel Hempstead and Isleworth, and it can be appreciated that, in Victorian terms, he was already a wealthy man.

And this is what he remained, despite various losses in 1866 (the side-effects of the great banking scandal of May that year, when Overend & Gurney, London's leading discount house, closed with liabilities of over ten million pounds). When he died in 1896 he left an estate valued at £63,590 2s 10d to be divided equally between his faithful sisters, Mary Victoria and Mary Sabilla.

Life during those thirty years at the Villa Novello passed in a pleasant round of literature and gardening. Mary and Charles Cowden Clarke wrote as avidly as ever, while Alfred and Sabilla devoted themselves to transforming the villa from a rather bleak, four-square block into a charming and luxurious home, surrounded by superb formal gardens overlooking the blue Mediterranean sea.

And when he was not engaged in 'improvements', Alfred gave his mind to engineering matters. He seems to have been, for a while at least, in partnership in an engineering business with a relative, Antonio Novello–the son, perhaps, of a half-forgotten cousin. He also applied himself to inventions of various kinds.

Evidence of his practical approach to life–the same approach that had made him so successful as a publisher–has already been given. It had led him into unexpected paths and the championship of unexpected causes. In 1850, for example, he had published at his own expense a singularly wise pamphlet entitled: '24 o'clock; A few words on the advantages of a DISTINCT NAME for EACH HOUR of the day', to be sold 'at all Railway Stations. Price One Penny'.[19] In it, set out with indisputable logic, he explained the advantages of the 24-hour clock. It has taken his fellow-countrymen more than a hundred years to reach the same happy conclusion.

A few years later, from Genoa, came details of the 'Novello-craft; a proposed method for accomplishing GREAT SPEED in journeying OVER WATER'. In this instance, though, it has to be conceded that the scheme (an ingenious system of rollers that was supposed to turn each boat into a kind of sledge) was not argued quite far enough to carry conviction at any period, even though it was 'not patented to any country, but open to the free use of all'.[20] From Genoa also, in a pamphlet dated February 1876, came outlines for a new type of craft, the 'Novello-Skimmer'. It seems to have worked, in miniature on the garden pond. But its practical application on the open sea and on a larger scale is another matter.

The style of his restless, eager mind can be gauged from a letter he wrote to his nephew Mario Gigliucci, then in charge of various mining activities on his father's estates:

Did I not formerly call your attention to the value of the *Wind* as a motive power? I think you might very well consider carefully whether you could not introduce it with great economy and advantage in connection with the labours to be accomplished at the mines . . . The Wind brings itself carriage free, and the motive power costs nothing but the diligence to use it whenever present . . .[21]

When Alfred Novello died, on 16 July 1896, he had been in retirement for forty years. During that time the firm he had built up from almost nothing had become one of the most powerful and influential in Europe. He had had the satisfaction of seeing that the choice of Henry Littleton as his successor had been wise beyond his wildest dreams. And though he cannot have guessed that in little more than two years his 'family' firm would go public, he must have been well assured that it would sail with confidence into the century that he himself would never see.

CHAPTER SEVEN

NOVELLO, EWER & COMPANY

Even in terms of sheer physical bulk, the difference between Novello catalogues issued at roughly either end of Henry Littleton's reign gives a vivid idea of the extent of his success. The first, published in April 1858, is a slim, oblong volume measuring 9½ inches by 3¾, elegantly bound in an embossed brown cloth and containing 196 pages printed in single column. It is divided into six main sections: organ music; sacred music with English words; music in separate vocal and instrumental parts; instrumental music; vocal music (secular); and sacred music with Latin words. Each section is further broken down into subsections; for example under section three the following are found: oratorios, odes, cantatas, festival hymns and anthems, operatic music and secular cantatas, overtures, symphonies and marches, madrigals, glees, Latin music and so on.

The variety of music on offer, though mainly vocal, is considerable and often very enterprising. Vincent Novello's hand is everywhere apparent, both as a composer and as the editor and arranger of other men's music. The three volumes of his *Select Organ Pieces* ('Music from the most Celebrated Writers of the German and Italian Schools arranged as Voluntaries')[1] can be had at a guinea-and-a-half a volume, or in eighteen books at 6s each, or even in 108 separate numbers, each at 1s 3d. A similar arrangement governs the two volumes of his *Cathedral Voluntaries* ('Music arranged as Voluntaries, from the most Celebrated Cathedral composers of the English School').[2]

But other editors have also put in an appearance. Thus Edward

Rimbault provides organ accompaniments for 'A collection of Ancient Church Music, originally printed for the Motett Society, consisting of Services and Anthems by the best English and Italian Composers'[3] (among others, Byrd, Tallis, Palestrina, Vittoria and Lassus), while the Revd Sir Frederick Gore Ouseley provides 'A collection of Cathedral Services, set to music by English Masters' (one of whom is the Revd himself!).[4]

Under sacred oratorios, retailing at prices ranging from 1s 6d to 4s when printed in octavo size and bound in paper, and 3s and 5s when bound in scarlet cloth with gilt lettering, are ten by Handel, as well as Beethoven's *Engedi*, Haydn's *Creation*, Mendelssohn's *St Paul* and Spohr's *Last Judgment*. English composers have also begun to make a tentative appearance in this part of the catalogue, for example Henry Hugo Pierson's *Jerusalem* and Sir Frederick Gore Ouseley's *The Martyrdom of St Polycarp* (not to mention the Revd Samuel Stephenson Greatheed's masterpiece, *Enoch's Prophecy!*).

The collection of purely instrumental music is, in comparison, decidedly limited. Sinfonias from various oratorios make an appearance, and so do Mendelssohn's *Hymn of Praise* symphony and Grand Concerto in D minor, but beyond this there is nothing. Under keyboard and chamber music the list is a little more exciting, enlivened by a complete set of Mozart piano sonatas, seven books of Mendelssohn's *Songs without Words* and a volume briefly entitled: 'The unpublished and rarely known works of John Sebastian Bach, for clavier or pianoforte, a collection of Toccatas, Fugues, Fantasias, etc., calculated to lead the student into the highest departments of clear and expressive execution; the fingering by Czerny, adapted to English use'. A 'Grand Sonata' by Dr Gleitsmann, with the somewhat chauvinistic title *The Fall of Paris*, represents a solitary excursion into the truly exotic, 'pertaining more to the style of Beethoven, than to the filigree work of modern composers' we are assured.[5]

A collection of Mozart's violin sonatas, piano trios, quartets and quintets, together with Mendelssohn's op.45 Cello Sonata (also available for violin and piano!) make up the entire chamber music catalogue, and 'A Grand Selection of Sacred Music' (culled mainly from Handel's oratorios) 'arranged, adapted, and dedicated to Her Most Gracious Majesty the Queen, by William Webb, late Master of the Band to the Vectis Light Dragoons' provides a solitary nod in the direction of the military band world.[6]

The 1893 catalogue is a very lavish affair. It measures 10½ inches by

7, and runs to 360 pages printed in double column. It is thus nearly four times the size of the 1858 catalogue. The contents, laid out along basically the same lines as before but with a more rational and clear-cut division between types of music, represent an enormous leap forward both in variety and quality. In little more than thirty years, everything the firm was hinting at seems to have come to fruition. Leaving aside the substantial increase in what we would now consider as established classics, but which were then novel and unproven quantities (Schumann, Berlioz, Liszt, Gounod, Dvořák, Niels Gade, Wagner and Verdi) the truly impressive aspect is the obvious willingness and wherewithal to encourage music by native composers. New English cantatas and oratorios, anthems and part-songs are there in abundance. But so too are new instrumental works: overtures, symphonies, concertos and even chamber music; full scores and orchestral parts excellently printed and readily available–an astonishing act of faith in the possibility of an English musical renaissance, and a positive encouragement towards its fulfilment.

Among the steps that led to this development (the details of which will be discussed at a later stage) perhaps the most significant was Henry Littleton's recognition that by himself he was not wholly equipped to guide the firm's music policy. Whereas Alfred Novello's list of publications had been heavily influenced by his father's tastes and enthusiasms, Littleton had nothing like that in his background. On taking over responsibility in 1861 he therefore promptly appointed the young Joseph Barnby (1838–96), a brilliant organist and aspiring composer (narrowly beaten into second place by an even more brilliant Arthur Sullivan in the struggle to gain the Royal Academy's first Mendelssohn Scholarship) as his music adviser. It was a shrewd move; and if Barnby's talents as a composer never fulfilled their early promise (he is now remembered, if at all, by the sentimental but effective part-song 'Sweet and Low', which Novello's found to be a very lucrative property), his general abilities as an all-round musician are not to be denied.

Barnby remained the firm's music adviser until 1875, during which time he acquired a particularly promising assistant, the Dutchman, Berthold Tours (1838–97). He was succeeded, briefly, by Sir John Stainer, who resigned after little more than a year, thus leaving the field entirely to Tours, who took up the post in 1877 and held it until his death.

Littleton was also lucky in his sons. Alfred Henry (1845–1914), named presumably in honour of Alfred Novello, proved to be reasonably musical and to have inherited his father's flair for business. He joined the firm in 1862, aged seventeen. Augustus James (1854–1942), joined in 1871, but being largely unmusical concerned himself with the book-binding and printing side of the business.

In all these appointments Henry Littleton followed the precedent set by the Novellos in giving youth its head. Much of the vigorous growth enjoyed by the firm in the second half of the nineteenth century can be directly attributed to this enlightened policy.

One of the first signs of his determination to expand the firm's activities came in the summer of 1867 when he acquired the stock, plates and goodwill of J. J. Ewer & Company, a firm of music sellers and publishers founded in 1823 and operating, at the time, from 87 Regent Street. In a letter to J. Alfred Novello, dated 7 June, Henry Littleton explained the terms of purchase, incidentally revealing that he was confident of maintaining the healthy profit margin that had made him the owner of Novello's: 'I am to pay £15,000 for Ewer's business. I have paid £2,000; another £1,000 is due on July 1st, and I then pay £3,000 every six months, without interest'.[7] Then, as D'Almaine & Co's stock had been offered for sale in May 1867 following the death of Thomas D'Almaine in 1866, Littleton goes on to explain the further acquisitions:

> I have bought at Dalmain's Bishop's Ed. of Handel's songs, duets, trios to about 1,400 plates at 1s 4d per plate. The sacred music sold for next to nothing, but popular songs and piano pieces fetched marvellous prices. 'Kathleen Mavourneen' as a song with pf. arrangements brought about £800...

The purchase of Ewer & Co put Novello's in possession of a whole series of Mendelssohn copyrights, including those of *Elijah*, the 'Scottish' Symphony, the *First Walpurgisnight*, the Violin Concerto and the ubiquitous 'Hymn for soprano, chorus and orchestra', *Hear my prayer*.

The prices originally paid for these copyrights (presumably in respect of Great Britain only) make interesting reading. In an agreement drawn up in November 1850 between Ewer & Co and Mendelssohn's widow, confirming the original sales, it seems that *Elijah* was purchased in June 1847 for £257 10s 0d; *Hear my prayer* (June 1845) was bought for £4; the incidental music to *A Midsummer Night's Dream* (excluding the Overture) for £47 5s 0d (February 1844); the 'Scottish' Symphony (October 1842) for £20; and the Violin Concerto (June 1845) for a mere ten guineas. Sets of six *Songs without Words* were bought variously at fifteen and twenty-five guineas, and the magnificent *Variations sérieuses* for eight guineas (November 1841).

On 20 February 1869 Littleton concluded an agreement with Mendelssohn's son Karl for a further seventeen pieces, including the eighth book of *Songs without Words* and the 'Reformation' Symphony, for the sum of £534 2s 0d. Significantly, the final book of *Songs without Words* was valued at £200, whereas the symphony went for half the price! But by this time there was scarcely an amateur or professional pianist in the whole of the British Isles that did not have Mendelssohn's piano pieces at his or her fingertips, and it did not require courage for a publisher to invest in them–the courage came in purchasing, as Littleton did, the less marketable chamber pieces.

In acquiring Ewer's and changing the firm's name to Novello, Ewer & Company, Littleton found himself with a problem he may not have foreseen; space. In June 1867 he announced that the business would be operated both from 87 Regent Street and the two Novello addresses: 69 Dean Street and 35 Poultry. But this must have been a very awkward arrangement, and in October it was announced that all West End business would be conducted from a completely new address, 1 Berners Street.

In fact the move did not take effect until December 1867. For a while the Dean Street address was abandoned, but business again increased so rapidly that the lease was renewed. Printing was moved from Dean's Yard to no. 69 itself, and no. 70 was taken on purely for the storage of engraved plates and stereos. This arrangement remained until the major changes of 1906, though in the meantime the city office was moved from Poultry to 80 and 81 Queen Street, Cheapside (1876), and 111–13 Southwark Street were taken on as additional premises for book-binding and printing (1878).

The New York office also underwent several changes of address and, though the exact details are almost impossible to ascertain, various metamorphoses suggest that it was extremely difficult to run an American branch smoothly from a distance. The original address at 389 Broadway appears in advertisements in *The Musical Times* until December 1857. There is then a gap until May 1858, when the address is given as 6 Astor Place, changing to 1 Clinton Hall, Astor Place in August 1858. This address was maintained until September 1863.

There then follows a gap of eight years in which, it must be supposed, there was no New York office.

A new address, 751 Broadway, appears in *The Musical Times* in November 1871, and it was presumably this branch that Alfred Henry Littleton was sent out to organize. By April 1873, however, Novello's seem to have handed their business over to an agent, J. L. Peters, 599 Broadway (843 Broadway, after May 1875), whose services were replaced in July 1877 by those of Ditson & Company, Boston, New York and Philadelphia. This arrangement lasted until 1884, when Novello's again took matters into their own hands, opening a branch office at 129 Fifth Avenue, and moving four years later to 21 East 17th Street.

Fortunately things in London were more tranquil. The move to Berners Street meant that it was now possible to operate and further expand a new side of the business that had come with the purchase of Ewer & Company: the Universal Circulating Music Library. Advertisements explain its scope and purpose:

This Library has been established according to the principles of the best Continental Institutions, and embraces every branch of Musical Literature up to the present time. Messrs Novello, Ewer & Co. have spared neither exertion nor expense in order to make the Library the most valuable, complete, and extensive in existence; and Subscribers may for the moderate Subscriptions mentioned below, procure the loan of all the principal Publications, practical and theoretical, of home as well as foreign production, and thus make acquaintance with the whole range of Musical Publications, both classical and ephemeral. Novello, Ewer & Co. have published a catalogue of the Library, containing a classified List of upwards of

65,000 WORKS

all of which are available for the use of Subscribers.
In addition to these, Subscribers are entitled to select any Music in Novello, Ewer & Co.'s stock, although it may not be included in the Library Catalogue.
Terms of Subscription: Two Guineas per annum.

Per Half-year	£1 5s 0d
Per Quarter	15s 0d
Per Month	8s 0d
Per Week	3s 0d

Town Subscribers will be supplied with Two Guineas' worth of

Music, which may be exchanged once a week.
Country Subscribers will be supplied with Four Guineas' worth of
Music, which may be exchanged twice a month.
At the end of their Subscription, Annual Subscribers are entitled to
select Music to the amount of Half-a-Guinea net.[8]

The Library, we are further told, is open 'from nine to six o'clock,
Saturdays excepted, when it closes at three',[9] and that the subscribers
themselves must pay the cost of postage and packing. As a wise
precaution 'to facilitate the transmission of Music to and from the
Library, and to prevent it from being rolled, every Subscriber must be
provided with a portfolio, which can be supplied by Novello, Ewer &
Co., price 1s 6d each'.[10]

The Circulating Library continued to function, in what seems to
then have been a recklessly generous manner, until September 1937,
when it was sold for £25, in a presumably somewhat dog-eared
condition, to the second-hand department of Foyle's Bookshop.

The year 1867 marked also the beginnings of another Littleton
enterprise aimed at extending the power and influence of Novello,
Ewer & Company. He suggested to Joseph Barnby that he should
organize a choir 'with a view to presenting at public performances the
best specimens of choral compositions, executed in the most finished
style'.[11] Such an undertaking, to rival if possible the work of Henry
Leslie's famous choir, would clearly be of great benefit to British
music and a comfort to the music-loving public, as well as being an
excellent means of further advertising the firm's wares.

The first concert took place on 23 May and included Bach's motet 'I
wrestle and pray', Barnby being a leading Bach enthusiast of the time.
Such was the success of this event and the one that closely followed it,
that a season of four concerts was announced for the following year.

The first of these, given on 29 January 1868, was devoted entirely to
the music of Mendelssohn and included several new Novello acquisitions: the music for *Athalie*, the 'Reformation' Symphony and the
'Trumpet' Overture. By the end of the season it was generally agreed
that Mr Barnby's Choir was a welcome and important addition to the
London musical scene.

Thus encouraged, the firm now entered upon a series of Oratorio
Concerts at St James's Hall, with Barnby's Choir setting out to
revitalize the ground left fallow by the Sacred Harmonic Society's
resolute lack of interest in new music of any kind. The first took place

on 5 February 1869 and consisted of a performance of Handel's *Jeptha*, with new accompaniments provided by the twenty-five-year-old Arthur Sullivan in the happy belief that the composer would necessarily have wanted extra brass and woodwind to complete his vision. (It is only fair to Sullivan to point out that, as the details of other Handel oratorios in the Novello catalogue show, he was not alone in lending the master a helping hand. Composers from Mozart to Ebenezer Prout had been in their time equally forward with their improving services!)

Four concerts were given in the first season, and nine in the 1869–70 season that commenced in the autumn. Though these included performances of Haydn's *The Seasons* and Bach's *St Matthew Passion*, the high spot was a performance of Beethoven's *Missa Solemnis* 'as written' and without the modifications hitherto thought necessary to make the work performable. An important feature of all these concerts was the use of continental pitch (435 cycles per second), in a vain attempt to counteract the general English tendency to let it soar. When, in 1879, it reached a crippling 455 cps Adelina Patti refused to sing at Covent Garden.

A third season of six Oratorio Concerts began on 15 February 1871, and a fourth, of ten concerts, in the following autumn. By now the choir had grown to 500 and the concerts had to be transferred to Exeter Hall in the Strand, home of the Sacred Harmonic Society itself.

The success of the Oratorio Concerts now encouraged Novello's to expand their catalogue of choral music, adding not only new works by young British and Continental composers, but introducing the more difficult masterpieces of the past into its ever-cheaper octavo range. Thus Bach's *St Matthew Passion* was added to the list, and promptly given in a sacred building (Westminster Abbey, with Barnby conducting) for the first time in this country (6 April 1871). In this way the B minor Mass, Beethoven's Ninth Symphony and Berlioz's *Grande messe des morts* joined the growing list.

Indeed, choral music could now be said to have gripped the nation. And when, in March 1871, the new Royal Albert Hall was opened, what more natural thing to be chosen for the ceremony than a majestic choral concert. The conductor for this occasion was Charles Gounod, already in England sheltering from the miseries of the Franco-Prussian War.

Though famous and greatly admired, Gounod does not seem to have attracted the interest of British publishers until Henry Littleton saw his potential. He suggested that a new work would be a splendid addition to the concert, and Gounod replied with a cantata that would represent the Spirit of France, temporarily (he trusted) crushed by a brutal invader. *Gallia*, the outcome, was an instant success, eclipsing Ferdinand Hiller's *Triumphal March* and Sullivan's patriotic cantata *On Sea and Shore*. Gounod's reputation in England was confirmed, and Henry Littleton had netted yet another money-spinning composer.

His value, however, was not to be fully realized until the publication of the oratorio *The Redemption* in 1882. In the meantime his relations with Littleton, and indeed with all English potential publishers, went through a very bad patch. The root of the trouble lay in Mrs Georgina Weldon, a talented but somewhat over-enthusiastic amateur singer and teacher into whose clutches Gounod had fallen in 1871. In November that year he found himself part of a curious ménage-à-trois, more artistic perhaps than venial, at Tavistock House (the former home of Charles Dickens) where Mrs Weldon proposed setting up a National Training School of Music.

Nevertheless at first Gounod's relations with Novello, Ewer & Company were everything he, and they, could have desired. In January 1871 Littleton had purchased the copyright of four songs for £200–twice the amount the composer was accustomed to receive from his French publishers. In July he took three more works, *Gallia, De profundis* and *O salutaris hostia*, and paid £320 for the privilege. He then offered to take eight songs, but with the option of either purchasing them outright at £20 each and a royalty of 4d on each copy sold, or for a 6d royalty and no down-payment. Gounod, it seems, agreed.

When the songs began to arrive, Littleton was dubious and decided to opt for the 6d royalty. Gounod was furious. He repudiated the deal and took legal action. Littleton, to ease the situation, gave in. But the dust had scarcely settled when another dispute arose, this time over the words of a duet, *La siesta*. Littleton had asked a friend, Dr Dulcken, to provide a translation, which he had set up in proof and sent to Gounod for approval. Gounod disliked it and promptly applied to Francis Turner Palgrave for a better version. When this arrived, Littleton and Joseph Barnby thought it not so good as Dr Dulcken's effort and refused to accept it.

At this point Gounod, angry with the whole race of publishers, began to express his opinions about music and musical conditions in letters to the press, and in articles. One such letter concerned a rumour published in the *Sunday Times* that he had offered a new three-act opera to the Théâtre Italien in Paris on condition that Georgina Weldon sang the leading part. This he refuted, but complained of the paper's remark that 'either M. Gounod is deceived in the lady's powers, or the general public have done her a grave injustice'.[12] Not so, said Gounod, the public have always responded to her remarkable talents and 'the applause after she has sung has drowned the hisses, but I have heard them with my own ears, and known from people friendly to me that the hissers have been sent by publishers and agents in London'.[13]

Behind all this, wielding the pen and dictating the course of action to the infatuated composer, stood Georgina Weldon. In a further letter to the press he stated that of the several 'former traders' (i.e. publishers) referred to by the press in commenting on his original accusations 'the name of one firm...was conspicuous by its absence', and promptly named it as 'a well-known and powerful name–Messrs. Novello, Ewer & Company'.[14] Henry Littleton, now thoroughly exasperated, sued for libel.

At the hearing Gounod again dragged up the dispute over the songs and the translation, and added that Littleton had tried to 'mulct' him over various sums of money. 'He knew', he declared, 'that war had nearly ruined me, and that my house had been burnt down: I could not, therefore, believe he could have bargained with me under the circumstances...'.[15]

Mr Justice Denman considered the matter (at some length, for the whole tangled proceedings were later printed verbatim in *The Musical Times* (July 1873) and ran to some 28,000 words), and pointed out to the jury that Mr Littleton did not wish to press for damages, but wished merely to clear his name from Gounod's grave imputations. In the end, Littleton was awarded damages–of £2.

Gounod was jubilant until it dawned on him that the words '40s, if it carries costs' meant that he would have to foot a bill of £100. Georgina declared that he should not pay, but rather go to prison. And for a while it seemed that this was what would happen, though it is hardly likely that Littleton relished the idea of being responsible for incarcerating one of Europe's leading composers. Fortunately Gounod's relatives stepped in and, to his immense chagrin, his mother-in-law paid the bill.

Mixed in with the legal wrangles was the undoubted fact that by this time Gounod was unpopular with the musical public at large and with the Royal Albert Hall Company in particular. In the flush of enthusiasm that followed the successful inaugural concert he had been asked to conduct a newly formed Royal Albert Hall Choral Society. Inevitably he tried to infiltrate Mrs Weldon into the concerts as a soloist, and equally inevitably gave more space to his own music and arrangements than to British composers. Three of the four concerts he directed lost money, and it was delicately hinted that resignation might be the best step. He was succeeded by Joseph Barnby, who immediately amalgamated the Oratorio Choir and the Royal Albert Hall Choral Society and proceeded with a successful series of subscription concerts. The new choral society became the basis of the present-day Royal Choral Society.

The success of the Barnby–Novello subscription concerts of 1872–3 led to the firm being asked to plan a series of daily concerts at the Albert Hall to accompany the International Exhibition of 1873. Each concert lasted about an hour, and no charge was made for the unreserved tickets. The series began on 14 April and continued until the close of the Exhibition on 31 October, with Joseph Barnby as the main conductor. Littleton seized on them as a golden opportunity to present new artists to the public, and provide a platform for new music by young British composers.

The International Exhibition series was followed by a new season of eleven Oratorio Concerts including important performances of Bach's *Christmas Oratorio*, Handel's *Theodora* and, for the first time in London, Sullivan's Birmingham Festival oratorio *The Light of the World*.

It was now that someone in the firm, probably Alfred Littleton, conceived the idea of a regular series of nightly concerts, to begin on 7 November 1874. They were planned on a weekly basis: Monday was to be a ballad concert; Tuesday, English music; Wednesday, a 'Classical' night; Thursday, oratorio; Friday, Wagner; and Saturday a 'popular' night. The conductors included Edward Dannreuther, Alberto Randegger, John Francis Barnett, the pianist William Henry Thomas and Joseph Barnby. Two choirs were engaged: one for the larger works, and the other, a more intimate group, for part-songs

The whole undertaking was vast and completely revolutionary. Nothing like it had ever been attempted, and nothing was to come near it until the advent of the present-day Promenade Concerts (1895), of which the Novello series is a clear ancestor.

In fact it proved impossible to carry the series beyond seven weeks in its original form. The losses were too great, even for Novello's to withstand. But a modified scheme, with concerts twice a week, continued until May 1875, with Verdi's *Requiem*, sung by a chorus of 1200 (ten times the number required by Verdi for the first performance) and conducted by the composer himself, as the crowning achievement.

It was not until 1885 that Novello's felt able to sponsor another series of concerts, and this proved to be their last. It took the form of two seasons of six Oratorio Concerts, conducted by Dr (later Sir) Alexander Campbell Mackenzie. Several of the firm's newest publications were given a hearing, including Gounod's *Mors et vita*, Liszt's *St Elizabeth*, Dvorák's *St Ludmilla*, Spohr's *Calvary*, Sullivan's *The Golden Legend* and Mackenzie's own masterpiece, *The Rose of Sharon*. But their story, and the story of all Novello's later nineteenth-century publications belong to another chapter.

CHAPTER EIGHT

THE CATALOGUE EXPANDS

The second half of the nineteenth century witnessed, as we have already noted, a remarkable increase in Novello publications. Merely to dip into the 1893 catalogue is to become almost giddy at the sheer profusion of what was available. Indeed, there is so much to choose from that the very richness was surely self-defeating. Did all those anthems and part-songs sell? Or was it that certain popular items underwrote the cost of maintaining the rest? But it seems that nothing was allowed to go out of print, save when a work was deliberately replaced by a new and improved edition. The market that Alfred Novello had so cleverly anticipated was, apparently, limitless. The 1893 catalogue contains 360 pages: the 1913 version, in the same format, is double the size! Both shed a fascinating light on the way in which British musical taste was developing at the promptings of the country's leading publisher.

The first section of the 1893 catalogue is devoted to organ music. Here one notes that *The Organ Works of J.S. Bach* made their appearance, in a ten-volume edition (later to be expanded to fourteen) edited by Dr J. F. Bridge and James Higgs and sold mostly at 3s a volume. For the less ambitious there are several collections of 'arrangements from the scores of the great masters'[1] by, for example, William Best (one of the great executants of the day), George Cooper, Henry Nixon, and John Hiles, whose *Short Voluntaries* 'adapted from the works of the great masters' runs to five volumes, or forty-two books containing over four hundred pieces. The list of 'original compositions for the organ'[2] runs to nearly two hundred numbers and includes the work of a considerable variety of young composers, many of them commissioned by Novello's. Stanford, Macfarren, Mackenzie, Guilmant, Rheinberger and the American Horatio Parker are among them.

The catalogue of harmonium music that follows consists mainly of arrangements of popular classics, with the occasional original piece thrown in for good measure. There are arrangements also for harmonium and piano, with and without other instruments, some of which must have sounded bizarre, for example the *Danse des sylphes* from Berlioz's *Damnation of Faust*. Piano and harmonium accompaniments are also offered for a number of large works, such as *Elijah, Messiah,* and *The Creation* 'to obviate the difficulty experienced by such Country Choral Societies as are unable to procure the assistance of an orchestra'.[3] Novello's, it seems, thought of everything!

The catalogue of church services contains twenty-five double-column pages, with another thirty-two devoted to anthems. These cover a very wide range of composers, from the Elizabethans to Novello's own commissions from living composers. The octavo series known as *The Parish Choir Book*, begun in 1866 and consisting by 1893 of some 134 items, must have been particularly stimulating to young British composers, and specially helpful to the growing number of choirs in churches up and down the country. For the first volume no fewer than forty-six settings of the *Te Deum* were commissioned from such composers as Macfarren, Barnby, Henry Smart and Gore Ouseley. The series, originally published under the patronage of the Ely Diocesan Church Music Society, continued until the early 1970s when it numbered some 1600 items. Thereafter the classification of all published music was gradually changed to suit the requirements of a computer.

The array of Novello anthems is, if anything, even more dazzling, and there is literally no Victorian composer, however modest his talents, who did not make a contribution. Pride of place, for the period, we would now probably ascribe to Samuel Sebastian Wesley (represented by two dozen major anthems), but there are many more composers, such as Walmisley, Stanford, Sullivan, Sterndale Bennett and Stainer, whose best work is not unworthy of Wesley's and who are here more than adequately represented. Nor were composers of earlier periods neglected. Byrd, Gibbons, Purcell, Blow, Pelham Humfrey, Attwood, Boyce and Croft are all here, available in neatly printed scores at prices ranging from 1½d to 6d or 8d, and, very occasionally, 2s or 3s. Anthems and services could also be purchased in collections, bound in cloth, and usually also in the form of separate vocal and organ parts. Among such collections are Attwood's *Cathedral Music*, Boyce's *Collection of Cathedral Music* (in three volumes, two guineas each), Boyce's *Services and Anthems* (four volumes, a guinea each), Clarke-Whitfield's *Services and Anthems*, Croft's *Thirty Anthems and Burial Service*, Gibbons's *Sacred Compositions*, Greene's *Forty Anthems*, Kent's *Services and Twenty Anthems*, Nares's *Twenty Anthems*, Ouseley's *Services and Anthems*, Purcell's *Sacred Music* (edited by Vincent Novello, in four volumes, 31s 6d each) and Walmisley's *Cathedral Music*. It is an astonishingly comprehensive range, scarcely to be matched by anything a publisher can carry today.

Hymn books and psalters also occupy a large part of the general catalogue. The first series of Sir John Stainer's *Christmas Carols, Old and New* made its appearance in 1867, and Edwin Monk's *Anglican Hymn Book* in the following year. The two volumes of Joseph Barnby's *Original Tunes to Popular Hymns* (some 142 of them) appeared in 1869 and 1883 respectively, and his *Hymnary* (which among other things contained Sullivan's 'Onward, Christian Soldiers') in 1872. The *Bristol Tune Book* was published in 1881, and Troutbeck's *Westminster Abbey Hymn Book* in 1883. Outstanding among the many psalters are Stainer and Barnby's *Cathedral Psalter*, Edwin Monk's *Anglican Chant Book* and the many publications of Thomas Helmore that the firm had begun to issue in 1848, including his *Primer of Plainsong, The Canticles Noted, The Psalter Noted* and *A Manual of Plainsong*.

No mention is made of *Hymns Ancient and Modern* in the 1893 catalogue, although Novello's were the printers when it first appeared in 1860. It was immediately and enormously successful and remained so throughout the century, until Vaughan Williams's *The English Hymnal* of 1906 challenged its supremacy. The manner in which it was printed was much admired, and Novello's were happy to run off the hundreds of thousands of copies that were sold in its first years. Unfortunately, early in 1869, a dispute arose over the ownership of certain copyrights. The exact details are hard to disentangle, but a statement of the year's accounts submitted by Henry Littleton's solicitors, Messrs Shaen & Roscoe, give, in dry legal shorthand, a reasonably clear picture of the situation. For example, on 11 February 1869, they made the following submission of their recent activities:

Conferring on letter received from Messrs Parke & Pollock solicitors for Proprietors determining your engagement as Publisher and advising thereon, conferring as to your rights as Proprietor of Copyright in works from which selection had been made by the compilers of Hymns A & M to forbid the future publication of that work in its present state.

Writing them accordingly accepting a determination of engagement on terms proposed and giving them notice that further publication of the work in its present state would be an infringement of your copyrights and would be followed by proceedings against the proprietor.[4]

By April it seems that Littleton had made up his mind to 'allow the publication of [his] copyright, if the proprietors of the collection would allow [him] to use a similar number of theirs'.[5] And presumably all would have been well had the solicitors not discovered that, by some oversight, he had forgotten to register himself as the owner of the copyrights he claimed! It is hardly surprising to find that the proprietors of *Hymns Ancient and Modern* immediately transferred the licence to print to Messrs Clowes, and Novello's had to forfeit a valuable contract.

They were, however, not short of work as the 1893 catalogue shows. Even if they had been concerned only with the fifty pages devoted to oratorios, cantatas, masses and operas, printed in 'Full Score, Vocal Score, Separate Vocal and Orchestral Parts, etc.',[6] it would have been enough to satisfy the average publisher. This was the real meat of their nineteenth-century empire and its fascination is endless. Here we see high Victorian taste at its most typical and most rampant. For here Novello's could offer no fewer than 736 individual works, from the industrious pens of 235 composers.

It is not so much the standard choral works of Handel, Haydn, Mozart, Beethoven, Schubert, Schumann, Spohr, Mendelssohn or even Berlioz that fascinate—at least they seem to have been mostly written under genuine artistic compulsion. But the plethora of oratorios and cantatas, sacred and secular, that popular demand elicited from British composers, good, bad and mediocre, is amazing. In their search for suitable subjects they plumbed the depths of Christian mythology and scoured the byways of literature. Scarcely a saint or martyr was left without the benefit of choral exegesis, scarcely a hero's exploits remained unsung. In its way, the Novello choral work was the 'pop' music of the nineteenth century's middle classes, and on the evidence of the catalogues one might well suppose that everyone from Land's End to John o'Groats was singing.

And the fact is that they probably were! If London audiences could delight in monster performances of Handel's *Messiah* at the Crystal Palace–in 1857 the choir and orchestra numbered 2500 and the 'Hallelujah Chorus', we are told, 'could be distinctly heard nearly half a mile from Norwood, and its effect, as the sound floated on the breeze, was impressive beyond description and sounded as if a nation was at prayers'–then it is scarcely likely that less favoured regions would be far behind.[7]

A glance at the programmes of three consecutive meetings of the Three Choirs Festival may demonstrate the part that Novello's played in all this choral jubilation. At Gloucester in 1880 the main new work was Parry's *Prometheus Unbound*, a Novello publication. Old favourites included *Elijah, The Last Judgment*, the *Missa Solemnis, Messiah* and Mozart's Requiem–all doubtless sung from the familiar buff brown Novello copies. At Worcester in 1881 the *Messiah* and *Elijah* again loomed large, together with *The Creation*, Beethoven's *Engedi*, and Cherubini's D minor Mass. Sir Alexander Campbell Mackenzie's cantata *The Bride* was the new Novello work. A similar selection enlivened the 1882 meeting at Hereford: the *Messiah, St Paul* and Bach's *Magnificat*, with Alice Mary Smith's *Ode to the Passions* and Dr Garrett's *The Shunamite* as the main novelties. At these three meetings the only works not published by Novello's were Henry Holmes's cantata *Christmas Day* (1880) and Alfred James Caldicott's 'sacred cantata' *The Widow of Nain* (1881). In other years, and at other festivals they were less remiss: the choral scene throughout the second half of the century was literally dominated by their publications.

The encouragement all this activity gave to young British composers can scarcely be over-estimated. In the choral field alone, Novello's published large-scale works by nearly every composer of importance, whether he was already established, or had just arrived on the scene. The fact that not all their efforts proved to be of lasting value is neither here nor there. What matters is the atmosphere of encouragement that was created, for out of their efforts came the men of true genius who were to rescue their country's music from the doldrums.

The list of the precursors is in itself impressive: John Francis Barnett and Julius Benedict; William Sterndale Bennett, whose copyrights in *The May Queen* and *The Woman of Samaria* Novello's acquired from

Leader & Cock (at £2000 and £500 respectively); Frederick Bridge and Frederic Cowen; Hamish MacCunn and George Alexander Macfarren; Alexander Mackenzie, J. B. McEwen, Hubert Parry and John Stainer; Charles Stanford and Arthur Somervell; and Arthur Goring-Thomas. Nor, if we are to be true to the period, can we overlook the enormously successful, if somewhat meretricious, work of Henry Gadsby and Alfred R. Gaul.

Even women composers make an appearance in the 1893 catalogue with substantial works: Ethel M. Boyce, Rosalind Ellicott, Charlotte Sainton-Dolby, Emma Mundella, Alice Mary Smith, and, finest of all, Ethel Smyth, whose powerful Mass in D is included. American talent, cut along strictly British lines however, also makes its bow in works by Dudley Buck, Frederick Converse and Horatio Parker (whose *Hora novissima* (1893) was popular enough to make him an Englishman by proxy).

However popular in their day (and in terms of contemporary sales very little of their music can be considered a publishing failure), the work of these composers has now faded. Parry's *Blest Pair of Sirens* has survived, and recent probings suggest there is much more to the rest of his work than fashion can yet admit. Stanford's cantata *The Revenge* also receives the occasional performance. Most impressive of all has been the durability, and apparent indestructibility, of Stainer's *Crucifixion*—a million and a quarter copies sold since its publication in 1887, and still in print!

Not that all the choral works of Novello's continental composers fared much better. Who now has time for Spohr's oratorios, or the choral works of Félicien David, Niels Gade, Hermann Goetz or Ferdinand Hiller—all famous in their day, and lucrative additions to the Novello catalogue. Nor have the oratorios of Dvořák, Gounod and Liszt enjoyed permanent favour, despite their composers' greater ability. However, it must be said that Dvorak's Mass in D, his *Stabat Mater* and Gounod's *Messe solennelle* still command healthy sales and regular performances.

Nevertheless, despite its ultimately ephemeral nature, it is evident that the Novello choral catalogue was both important and influential in the second half of the nineteenth century: characteristic of period taste to a degree that no other English publisher could match. In many respects it *was* the music of Queen Victoria's reign.

Exactly how popular such pieces were can be gathered from the sales figures of the period. The only stock book that has survived covers the years 1858–69, but it gives a clear indication of the way things were going. The octavo edition of Handel's *Messiah*, for example, sold an average of 6500 copies a year. Haydn's *Creation* comes second with a sale of 3600, and Handel's *Judas Maccabaeus* and Mendelssohn's *St Paul* tie for third place with an annual sale of 2850. Then come *Israel in Egypt* (1800), *The Seasons* (1250) and Beethoven's Mass in C (1000). A minority publication, such as Berlioz's *Treatise on Instrumentation*, took ten years to sell its first 1000 copies!

In their search for new works Novello's were not afraid to pay handsomely, especially when it came to tempting important foreign composers into the fold. Of these, Gounod was certainly the most successful in holding out for a just reward. In the case of his oratorio *The Redemption*, there were many who said that his demands were outrageous, and that in agreeing to them Henry Littleton had taken leave of his senses. Planned as early as 1867, the oratorio, or 'sacred trilogy' as Gounod liked to call it, was given its first performance at the Birmingham Festival of 1882. For this privilege, and presumably 'anxious for to shine in the high aesthetic line', the Festival Committee had agreed to his demand for the unprecedented sum of £4000 which, in fact, would give them world rights in its future performance. Inevitably they got cold feet as soon as they realized what they had done, and turned to Henry Littleton for help. He agreed to take over the copyright for £3250, leaving the festival to pay the balance in respect of the first performance and Gounod's personal appearance as conductor.

The gamble paid off handsomely. The work was an enormous success, both at Birmingham (where two performances had to be given) and throughout the rest of the world. It was accepted on all sides as the great religious masterpiece of the century; immortality was prophesied, and the sales were immense. Littleton made a clear profit and had the satisfaction of seeing his sceptical fellow publishers confounded. Gounod, who had done everything in his power to make the work a success, including a prudent change of dedication which deleted his mother in favour of Queen Victoria, doubtless felt a certain vexation at having played into the hands of the man who had once taken him to court.

But evidently the irritation did not fester, for three years later Littleton struck another lucrative bargain with him over the oratorio *Mors et vita*, which received its first performance at the Birmingham Festival of 1885. This time Gounod was not able to direct it in

The Novello Family and their friends. Oil painting by Edward Petre Novello, *c.* 1831

1. Sabilla Novello 2. Mrs Blaine Hunt 3. Charles Cowden Clarke 4. Mary Victoria Novello (Mrs Cowden Clarke) 5. Alfred Novello 6. Florence Novello 7. Clara Novello
8. Cecilia Novello (Mrs Serle) 9. Vincent Novello 10. Edward Holmes 11. Charles Stokes
12. Edward Novello 13. Emma Novello 14. Mrs Mary Sabilla Novello

Vincent Novello. Oil painting by
Edward Petre Novello, c. 1834

Mary Sabilla Novello at the time of
her marriage. Miniature by James
Holmes, 1808

J. Alfred Novello, aged nineteen.
Miniature by Edward Petre
Novello, *c.* 1830

Henry Littleton.
Daguerreotype, 1856

Clara Novello. Pencil and chalk
sketch by Edward Petre Novello,
c. 1834

Villa Quaglia, Nice. Pencil and chalk sketch, *c.* 1860

Villa Novello, Genoa, photographed in 1874

Westwood House, 1886: The exterior
                     The music room

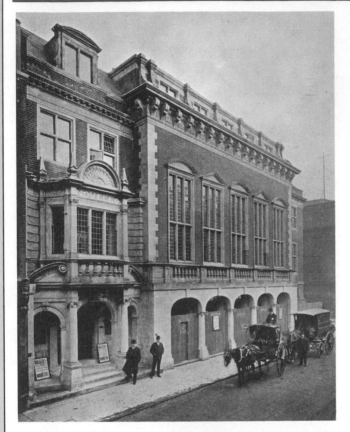

Wardour Street, 1906:
The exterior

The interior
The Sales Hall

Printing machinery in the Wardour Street factory

Present-day printing at Borough Green

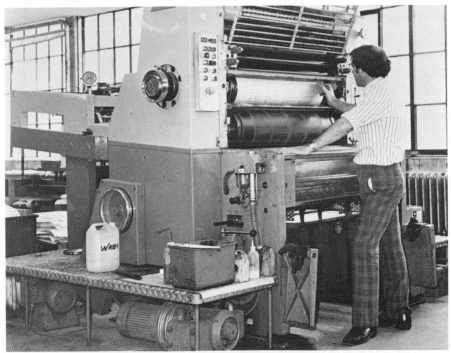

CRYSTAL PALACE.

THE PUBLIC, VISITING THE CRYSTAL PALACE, are invited to inspect the Specimens of Printing, &c. exhibited by J. ALFRED NOVELLO, in the Stationery Court.

The letters on the front of the above case offer some interest as specimens of Typography. The word

NOVELLO's

is formed of many thousand letters in Clarendon Brevier Capitals, detailing some of the peculiarities of cheap music. The word **CHEAP** is formed of Type Borders and Flowers. The word **MUSIC** contains the melody and words of "Rule Britannia," in the beautiful Pearl-Nonpareil Music Type, which belongs exclusively to the Dean-street Establishment.

J. Alfred Novello, London and New York.

The Novello stand at the Crystal Palace Exhibition, as reproduced in a *Musical Times* advertisement, 1854

Above right Detail of the stand's lettering, 'C'

Below right The Westminster Abbey memorial window

person—he was too busy evading a writ of debt that the importunate Georgina Weldon had issued against him! The box office receipts were even greater than before, and Littleton's payment for the world copyright (the same as he had paid for *The Redemption*) was once more justified. Not everybody was pleased, however. Even the kindly and modest Dvorák was disturbed and, in October 1884, wrote to Littleton:

> That you were in Paris you have written to me, but that you have bought the new oratorio 'Life and Death' by Gounod for the nice sum of 100,000 francs I got from the Wiena and Prague papers only yesterday. Pray do not pay Mr Gounod who truly does not need it so immense sums, for what would be left for me?[8]

What was left for his works, though generous enough, was rather closer to the average payment of the day. Dvorák had come to England for the first time in 1884 when, in conjunction with the Philharmonic Society, Novello's invited him to conduct his *Stabat Mater* at the Albert Hall. His music had already made a considerable impression in England, and the success of the 1884 visit turned him into a composer that choral festivals wished to encourage. Accordingly, for the 1885 Birmingham Festival he wrote the cantata *The Spectre's Bride*, and for the 1886 Leeds Festival the oratorio *St Ludmilla*. In 1891 his Requiem received its first performance at the Birmingham Festival. For the British copyright in these works Novello's paid £200 for *The Spectre's Bride*, £250 for the *Stabat Mater* and £650 for each of the other two.

Much the same was done in the case of the Danish composer Niels Gade, who visited England for the first time in 1876 and whose choral works rapidly became favourites with the societies. Writing to Henry Littleton on 19 October 1881, he outlined plans for a new cantata, *Psyche*, which he was writing for the Birmingham Festival, and asks 100 guineas for the British copyright. Littleton, answering almost by return, saw no reason to quibble.

British composers fared, on average, slightly less well. Many seem to have been content to let their works go for very small sums; sometimes, in the case of short pieces such as part-songs, merely in return for fifty copies for their own use. Stainer's acceptance, in June 1887, of a 2d royalty on each copy of the *Crucifixion* is fairly typical—though in his case the rewards were to go far beyond what most composers could expect. In 1868 we find Samuel Sebastian Wesley disposing of a collection of twelve works, including the anthems *Cast me not away*, *Wash me throughly*, *The Wilderness* and *Ascribe unto the Lord*, for £750 and clearly feeling that he had done well. 'When I get home', he is reported to have said, 'they'll think I've been robbing somebody!'.[9] In December 1876, Sullivan, a more than averagely keen businessman, asks 100 guineas for six anthems; while in March 1884 Alexander Mackenzie, a great favourite with the Littletons, is given £500 for the copyright in *The Rose of Sharon*.

What these sums signify in present-day terms is difficult to estimate. But it is worth noting that an apprentice, one Henry Clark, indented on 24 June 1874 as a letter-press printer had to be content with 7s a week in his first years, with the prospect of rising to 21s after a seven-year apprenticeship. A letter of complaint from a fully-fledged engraver (evidently one of several recruited by Henry Littleton in Leipzig in 1876) makes the point even more clearly:

> April 27th, 1878.
> Dear Sir,
>   I beg to tell you that I shall leave my situation in your office on Saturday the 4th of May. The reason is I cannot live with 45 shillings a week and because I cannot agree with Mr Brause. None of the other engravers can agree with him, as you can easily hear from them.
>   This is the principal reason why I want to leave and I shall tell you more about it if you wish it.
>   yours sincerely,
>   Hugo Hornmann.[10]

The reply, sketched in pencil on the back, was prompt and decisive and couched in terms that nowadays would probably signal a strike:

> Herr Hornmann –
>   Received your letter this morning stating that you wish to leave on Saturday next, May 4th.
>   I have every confidence in Herr Brause and feel sure that if any disagreement has taken place the fault has not been with him. I have heard that for some time you have not worked in a way satisfactory to Mr Brause and have no doubt that had you not decided to leave I should have been very shortly compelled to give you notice myself.

You are aware that you are indebted to me to the sum of
£3 15s 0d which I paid you as vorschluss.* I shall be glad to know
how and when you propose to pay this.
                    Henry Littleton.[11]

In 1980 the minimum union rate for an engraver of Mr Hornmann's
standing was £94 a week.

Even assuming that relative money values do not necessarily involve a multiplication factor of forty-two, or thereabouts, it can be
seen that in nineteenth-century terms the fees that Henry Littleton was
prepared to pay for his copyrights were remarkably generous, and in
Gounod's case (£168,000?) almost foolhardy.

Though vocal music dominates the 1893 catalogue, the few pages
devoted to orchestral and chamber music indicate that the firm had
become aware of a duty to encourage the efforts of British composers
in these fields, even if the returns at this date must have been meagre.
Only four pages are given over to orchestral music, but they contain
several significant names. Among the printed full scores—magnificently produced, and beautifully engraved in folio size—are symphonies by
Frederic Cowen (no. 4, 'The Welsh'), Oliver King (Symphony in F,
'Night'), Ebenezer Prout (Symphony in F), and Charles Stanford
(Symphony no. 3, the 'Irish', and Symphony no. 4, in F). There are
also concert overtures by Frederick Corder, *Prospero*, Oliver King,
Among the Pines, Hamish MacCunn, *The Land of the Mountain and the
Flood*, and Sullivan, *Di ballo* and *In Memoriam*, concertos by Mackenzie
and Stanford and a symphonic poem, *La belle dame sans merci*, by
Mackenzie. Available in manuscript are works by Edward German
and Frederick Cliffe (Symphony in C minor), and, most significantly
of all, Edward Elgar, whose concert-overture *Froissart* had been
accepted for publication in 1890.

Add to this a complete edition of Schubert's symphonies, a fine
selection of Mendelssohn's orchestral works, sinfonias from Handel's
oratorios, Beethoven's Choral Fantasia and Ninth Symphony, and
Dvořák's Symphony no. 4 (acquired in 1891 for £100, after the
composer's quarrel with Simrock), and it can be seen that the firm was
beginning to make bold strides in a new direction.

The chamber music section, however, is very small indeed, but it
contains string quartets by W. H. Hadow, John Mee and Carl Toms,

---

* Vorschuss, the word Littleton wanted, means 'an advance'.

together with George Alexander Macfarren's Third Piano Sonata, cello sonatas by Walter Macfarren, Hubert Parry and Charles Stanford, a violin sonata and piano trio by Stanford and a piano quartet by Parry. Some of these, however, seem to have been published as 'author's property'.

A very considerable section of the catalogue is devoted to books of instruction covering most aspects of musical theory and performance. The series of music primers, begun in 1877, already numbers forty volumes, ranging from François Fétis on *Choir Training and Choral Singing* to John Curwen on *Tonic Sol-fa*, James Higgs on *Fugue*, and John Stainer on *Harmony* and *Composition*. The series had a valid life well into the twentieth century.

Under the heading 'musical literature' are to be found translations of Philip Spitta's *Johann Sebastian Bach*, Otto Jahn's *Life of Mozart*, Dr Eduard Hanslick's *The Beautiful in Music* and Mauritz Hauptmann's *Letters of a Leipzig Cantor*. Books by English writers are, if anything, even more adventurous, and include Margaret Huggins's *Giovanni Paolo Maggini*, Edward Holmes's *Life of Mozart*, J. Fuller Maitland's *English Carols of the Fifteenth Century*, Stainer's *Music of the Bible* and a lavish edition of Captain Day's monumental *The Music and Musical Instruments of Southern India and the Deccan*.

The section devoted to glees, madrigals, part-songs and opera choruses contains forty-two pages and includes a three-volume edition of Sir Henry Bishop's works, twenty volumes of the Novello Part-Song Book, a new series for male voices called *Orpheus* (seven volumes, so far), a seven-volume collection of trios and quartets for female voices, and literally thousands of individual pieces covering the entire range of British madrigal, glee and part-song, from the Elizabethans to the end of the nineteenth century, and selling at prices ranging from a 1½d to 6d for the octavo editions, and a little more for the now dwindling stock of folio editions.

Solo, duet and trio songs are on offer, with English, French, German and Italian words. Among the solo songs are collections of Beethoven, Brahms, Charles Dibdin, Dvořák, Robert Franz, John Liptrot Hatton, Haydn, James Hook, Edward James Loder, George Alexander Macfarren, Alexander Mackenzie, Mendelssohn, Mozart, Rubinstein, Schubert (seven volumes), Schumann and Tchaikovsky.

The oldest part of the catalogue comes next: sacred music with Latin words—much of it the result of Vincent Novello's enthusiasms. The newest part completes the catalogue: Novello's 'Tonic Sol-fa Series', which offers nearly eight hundred works in this form, including over sixty large-scale sacred works, and a similar number of secular pieces— everything, in fact, from Handel's *Messiah* to *The Golden Legend* of Sir Arthur Sullivan.

The range of Novello publications cheaply available at the end of the nineteenth century was not only vast, but well calculated to satisfy the needs of every aspect of British music-making. With something like twelve thousand octavo works in print, and another ten thousand in folio or other sizes, it was the most magnificent collection that any British publisher could offer. And having correctly assessed the tastes of the century, Novello's were now quietly moving in a new direction —towards the bias of the twentieth century, orchestral music.

CHAPTER NINE

NOVELLO & COMPANY LIMITED

In the process of turning Novello, Ewer & Company into the wealthiest and most influential British music publishing house of the day, Henry Littleton had also made himself a very rich man. By 1874 he was ready to demonstrate the extent of his achievement in the kind of personal terms that Victorians would understand. For the sum of £12,000 he purchased a farm house and land on the southern slope of West Hill in fashionable Sydenham, and there he went to live. Writing from Italy on 28 April 1876 Mary Cowden Clarke gives a brief but telling picture of what this first version of 'Westwood House' must have been like:

> My last letter from my sister Cecilia gave an enchanting account of your new farm. Shouldn't I like to be snugly installed in the 'Lodge-cottage' she describes, and feed the chickens for you! Tell Mrs Littleton, when she goes there I hope she'll think of me and of how much I should like to be with her. [1]

She wrote again on 5 May:

> How I should enjoy some of those '150 eggs per week' with you and Mrs Littleton! Duck eggs are a special dainty, to my taste. A breakfast at the farm, on a spring morning, with you and Mrs Littleton, and a walk round the premises afterwards together, to see the lovely English scenery and the 5 Alderney beauties, and to see the meadows where sheep and pigs are probably to disport

themselves, wd. be a perfect feast to me! Well, I enjoy it in imagination; and it is at least delightful to know that *you two* dear friends wd. not dislike to have *us two* enjoying it with you in reality.[2]

But, even at £12,000, a farm and its attendant acres and rural delights were scarcely sufficient proof of having arrived, especially if you had had to work your way from the lowest rung. Something grander was needed. Henry Littleton therefore turned to one of the finest architects of the time, John Loughborough Pearson, and commanded that the existing buildings should be extended and remodelled and generally made into a memorial worthy of his upward climb.

Pearson, presumably as a pleasant change from the churches and cathedrals in which he specialized, chose to carry out his work in red brick and the general style of a French château. Soon gables and turrets and tall chimneys sprouted everywhere. A bell-tower was proposed, and ornamental conservatories grew like crystal mosques. There were spacious windows with heads of the great composers set in stained glass medallions, not to mention coats-of-arms drummed up by loyal genealogists who had contrived to find links with a twelfth-century Sir Henry de Littleton! Flights of stone steps led to terraces and ornamental gardens. It was altogether a fine effort in architectural bravura, and very theatrical.

Westwood House, to use the language of the Eastman Bros. when they came to sell it in April 1895, was 'a noble and imposing freehold mansion'. It was approached through 'an Avenue Carriage Drive, with Ornamental lodge at the entrance', and contained 'seventeen Bed and Dressing rooms, three fitted Bathrooms, handsome outer and inner Entrance Halls, a charming Double Drawing Room (about 55 ft in length, divided by a partière), Dining Room (30 ft by 30 ft), Morning Room or Boudoir, Library and Billiard Room combined (about 40 ft in length), and a magnificent Music Salon or Ball Room'.[3]

It was this last extravaganza that really caused mouths to gape. Panelled throughout in teak, with four massive columns supporting the wood-panelled ceiling, and a handsome fireplace 'chastely carved in Carrara marble' and resembling a family tomb, it measured 60 ft by 30 ft, and its walls were 16 ft high. It could seat 300 people, and the acoustics are said to have been exceptional. It was to this rural retreat that Henry Littleton welcomed the Abbé Liszt in 1886 on his last visit to England, and here that many another composer came to marvel at his publisher–host's success and ponder the extent of his own rewards.

The new Westwood House was declared open on 9 July 1881, with a 'Congratulatory ode' by the Revd Troutbeck (music by William Sewell, the 1879 Novello Scholar at the Royal Academy of Music), and a series of concerts. Kalozdy's Hungarian Band played during the afternoon, and the London Vocal Union, under the direction of Frederick Walker, sang glees and part-songs (Novello publications) at six o'clock.

> These goodly doors are open wide,
>   A welcome new to give;
> But first let Him be magnified
>   In Whom alone we live.
> The skill to plan, to raise, to deck,
>   These strong and stately walls,
> Which long may time lack power to wreck,
>   For heartfelt praises calls.[4]

trilled an unnamed tenor (probably Mr Walker) in blissful ignorance of what the future held.

Further celebratory concerts followed on 16 and 23 July, while on 25 July the Littleton family and their friends, including Sabilla Novello and Mary Cowden Clarke, staged an elaborate performance of *The Rivals*.

The glory of Westwood House is no more. The polished oak floors and solid mahogany doors, the 'valuable old Persian tiles' in the two best bathrooms, the embossed leather wall-papers, the ornamental Palm House, the Cucumber and Melon House, the Orchid House and the lean-to Vinery, the Gas Engine House and the Electric Light Accumulator House have all been swept away. It had cost Henry Littleton an estimated £50,000 to create the mansion, yet at his death it was purchased by a Mr Rabbitts, who promptly went into a decline, and the house was finally sold at auction, in 1899, to the National Union of Teachers Orphanage for a mere £10,000, having lain empty and neglected for nearly five years. Over the rolling acres, once 'secluded and finely timbered', are now dotted innumerable modern villas, patios and transistor radios, instead of music-rooms and Liszt's enchanted fingers.

Henry Littleton died on 11 May 1888. He was sixty-five and had enjoyed little more than a year of retirement. It is said that the sudden death of his daughter Cecilia, in 1885 had seriously undermined his health and made the struggle which had been his whole life seem futile. But true to form, he had made careful provision for his firm's future.

On 29 December 1886 he had concluded an agreement handing over Novello, Ewer & Company to his two sons, Alfred Henry Littleton and Augustus James Littleton, and to the husbands of his daughters Elizabeth Anne and Amy Eliza–George Topham Strangways Gill and Henry William Brooke. With Alfred Henry in supreme command, and Augustus as his second, and with provisions that effectively prevented George Gill and Henry Brooke or their heirs from usurping their authority, the four men became directors of the firm. In return he was to be guaranteed an annual income of £7000 for life, and his wife, should she survive him, half that sum. Thus, by the time of his unexpected death, the firm was already safely in practised hands.

So few personal documents have survived that it is hard to draw any conclusions about Henry Littleton's character and personality. That he was a man of extraordinary energy and courage is obvious. Later portraits show him patriarchal and bearded–almost indistinguishable from J. Alfred Novello. But a daguerreotype of 1856 tells a different story. Henry Littleton fixes the camera with a bold, determined gaze: the mouth is firm and the chin defiant. This is every inch a man intent upon winning.

Yet, for all the innocent grandeur of his final home, he seems never to have tried to disguise his humble origins. He liked to tell stories of his early struggles. He was never ashamed that his first contacts with music publishing had been confined to sweeping the floor–the malicious Gounod always referred to him as 'the old sweep'. His manners, it seems, remained blunt. Pestered by reporters on his arrival in America in 1877 as to whether he had come to extend his firm's business (he had, of course) he replied that he had merely come 'to see the bloody country'.[5]

One of the few vivid anecdotes of his later life is to be found in a letter written in 1894 by his neighbour Sir George Grove–another self-made man, but one that was uneasy about his social status. Grove recalls how he was invited to a fancy-dress party at Westwood House, and went disguised as an African chief:

> I found old L. (one of the vulgarest old snobs imaginable) sitting
> in his hall to receive his guests, with a large visitor's book on the
> table by him. I walked up to him and began "O great sage I have

come from the ends of the earth to enjoy your hospitality and taste the flavour of your wisdom, deign to utter a few words of welcome to your slave." I never saw a man look so bewildered. "Oh shut up, shut up," he said, "tell us 'oo you are." On which I took up the pen and fortunately recollected Persian enough to write a long name in the book.[6]

Even without the aspirates, Littleton emerges the better man.

In his *Musical Times* obituary Joseph Bennett concluded:

He was not a man of business in the hard, unsympathetic sense of the term. Few in his position ever allowed sentiment to influence them in an equal degree, or were capable of making sacrifices for an idea... A now prominent cathedral organist tells how, when comparatively an obscure man, he showed the Berners Street chief a work and named a certain price, only to have it doubled on the spot... Our dead friend had, in deed and in truth, a generous nature...Those who served him in a liberal spirit were liberally treated in return.[7]

Exactly how musical he was must remain in some doubt. Unlike members of the Novello family he was not a practising musician; but he clearly had a good nose for music and a very precise instinct for what would sell. And, as we have seen, he was not afraid to back his judgment with substantial sums of money. He reaped his rewards because he was willing to take risks.

He was, moreover, always eager to experience at first hand the latest developments in music. For example, he attended the first Bayreuth Festival in 1876 (he went with his son Alfred to the second cycle of *Ring* dramas). And if this seems unadventurous, it is worth remembering that Parry, who was at the same performances, had been assailed by his teacher, Sir George Macfarren, professor at Cambridge and principal of the Royal Academy of Music, with heartfelt pleas and dire warnings:

I am sorry you are going to Bayreuth, for every presence there gives countenance to the monstrous self-inflation. The principle of the thing is bad, the means for its realisation preposterous. An earthquake would be good that would swallow up the spot and everybody upon it, so I wish you were away.[8]

Littleton, the non-musician, was at least open-minded; though, business-like as always, he used the trip to engage new engravers in Leipzig and call upon Brahms in the hope of persuading him to write for the British oratorio market.

With the death of Henry Littleton no real change came over the running of Novello, Ewer & Company. Both Alfred and Augustus, now forty-three and thirty-four respectively, were in their prime and had enjoyed authority from their teens. George Gill (1846–1914) had joined the firm in April 1874 as manager of the printing department, shortly before his marriage to Annie Elizabeth Littleton; and Amy Eliza's husband, Henry Brooke (1848–1929), had joined in 1873, three years before their marriage. The articles of partnership had been supplemented on 31 December 1889 by the addition of Henry Reginald Clayton, who joined the board as company secretary on payment of a premium of £10,000. Under this management the firm prepared to launch itself into the twentieth century.

But the last years of the old century presented problems. The firm was scattered around London in various premises whose leaseholds were all due to expire by 1906, or thereabouts. Commonsense suggested that something should be done to rationalize the situation.

The first step was taken in 1897 when Novello's acquired from the Commissioners of Her Majesty's Woods and Forests an eighty-year leasehold on a group of old buildings running from Hollen Street to Little Chapel Street, with an entrance on to Wardour Street at no. 160. Here they proposed to erect a factory and provide a home for the printing, bookbinding and storage side of the business. This would enable them to vacate 69 and 70 Dean Street, and 112–14 Oxford Street, which they were using for storage. Frank Loughborough Pearson, the son of the architect who had created Westwood House and who was now Alfred Littleton's son-in-law, was commissioned to design the building, which was to be completed at a cost of £25,962 3s 4d (in the event it cost rather more than £32,000). It was also known that the leases on 152, 154, 156 and 158 Wardour Street would soon fall in and it would be possible to develop the site as a showroom and offices, thus enabling the firm to leave Berners Street as well. What the final cost would be, nobody yet knew; but it was clear that a considerable capital sum would have to be raised. The solution was to become a limited company.

The subscription list for shares in Novello & Company, Limited opened at ten o'clock on the morning of 26 April 1898. Out of a declared capital of £270,000, divided into 13,500 cumulative preference shares of 4½ per cent, and 13,500 ordinary shares of £10, preference shares to the value of £90,000 were on offer to the public. The ordinary shares were issued as fully paid to the five directors: 5062 to Alfred Littleton, 3796 to Augustus; 1899 each to George Gill and Henry Brooke, and 844 to Henry Clayton. The remaining preference shares were also bought in by them, Alfred taking 2250, Augustus 128, George Gill 1500 and Henry Brooke 615.

The prospectus, drawn up by Messrs Deloitte, Dever, Griffiths & Company, sets out the business and valuation of the firm in the following terms:

> We find that no account has ever been taken of the machinery and plant, nor has stock been taken of the music, etc., in hand, the profits always having been dealt with irrespective thereof. Subject to the above observation, we find that the available profits, after charging all expenses and the cost of acquisition of many copyrights, have, during the five years ending the 31st December, 1897, exceeded £100,000, or an average of £20,000 per annum.[9]

A valuation carried out by the printers Messrs Harrild & Sons, placed book debts at £34,535 2s 0d, stocks of books and music, white paper, binders' material, and work in hand (all taken at cost) at £34,861 12s 0d, cash in hand at £2,480 7s 9d, stereotyped and engraved plates at £81,685 13s 2d, plant and machinery, furniture and fittings at £40,421 10s 9d, and trade debts at £12,138 12s 5d. This left £88,154 5s 11d as the neat, accountant's valuation of copyrights, goodwill and leases, bringing the total to the required £270,000. By 29 April, 262 aplications for 18,380 cumulative preference shares had been received and the company was safely launched.

The minutes of the directors' meetings, beginning on 13 April 1898, make leisurely reading in the early years. The first problem to raise its head was that of staff wages. The board considered its payroll: 140 men and women employed in the printing and binding works, 84 in the two offices (Berners Street and Queen Street), 6 on pension—a total of 230 dependants. They braced themselves, agreed in principle that wages were too low, and made a start by increasing the £4 they paid August Jaeger (head of the publishing office) to a weekly £5. They then seem to have quietly shelved the matter.

For the most part they were required to deal only with trivial problems. We learn, for example, that one of the staff had managed to lose £6 from his cash by 'giving change for a cheque for that amount to an unknown customer, whose cheque [he] had subsequently lost', and that a further £1 was missing which he could not explain.[10] The board decided (20 March 1899) to swallow the story of the cheque, but ordered him to repay the missing £1 and warned him that the next lapse would mean the sack. On 23 April 1900 we learn that an outbreak of fire in Dean Street had been doused by the prompt action of Stoker White. He was congratulated on his vigilance and given £5, with a further £5 from a grateful insurance company. In October 1901 it seems that a forewoman in the binding works 'who had been in the company's service for many years, during which time she had unfortunately given way to intemperance, and that having been found drunk on the premises on three occasions she had been dismissed',[11] was now in need of help. The sum of £20 was set aside for her maintenance, to be prudently administered in payments of £1 a week.

In October 1902, however, a more serious matter arose. The board was shocked to find that Leipzig printers could offer more competitive prices than their own. It seemed that the new 209-page Prout edition of *Messiah* would cost £104 6s 3d in Germany, as against £179 16s 10d in Hollen Street, while sixteen-page anthems worked out at more than double the German price. Resolutions were passed that Novello & Company, Limited must 'reorganise and become competitive'.[12]

By 1904 the directors' minds were again on higher things. Leases were now falling in and decisions had to be made. On 20 January a building lease was signed for the Wardour Street site (nos. 152–8) that had taken their fancy when the factory was being built. It was for eighty years and at a ground rent of £385 per annum. By September the old buildings had been pulled down, and by January 1905 the Office of Woods and Forests had passed the plans drawn up by Frank L. Pearson. Work on the new showroom and offices now began.

At first the board entertained hopes of completing the building for £14,000. But Mr Pearson's estimate came to £19,200. This was revised to £18,500, and then reduced to £17,014–presumably by his agreeing to do without the series of symbolic statues he had intended to plant along the facade! Messrs Macey & Sons were engaged as builders, with Martyn & Co. retained to 'decorate the main hall'.[13]

This last expenditure, of £2750, prompted Henry Clayton into one of the few lengthy statements he ever made at a board meeting. He 'could not see the necessity of furnishing a room which would be used for the purpose of a shop in the fashion of an Banqueting Hall' and 'strongly felt that [it] should be completed after the style of a well-ordered shop'.[14]

But this is not what his fellow directors had in mind. Well-ordered and commercial Novello & Company, Ltd might hope to be, but it also stood for something more elevated and deserved to be presented to the world in a fitting manner. Memories of Westwood House came flooding back, and the banqueting hall theme won the day.

When the premises were opened to the public on 26 November 1906, it was found that the Art of Music had indeed been honoured. Novello's was the most sumptuous and splendid music shop that London had ever seen–a cathedral to Victorian enterprise and Edwardian self-satisfaction.

The new block added 776 square yards to the factory site of 1864 square yards. Pearson had turned to the Renaissance for inspiration, and to the Hanseatic town hall in particular (described by Pevsner as 'a remarkably original piece of scholarly adaptation', probably based on the Rathaus at Bremen (1612)).[15] The main entrance, on Wardour Street, consisted of an open porch of Portland stone, with three arches and a projecting balcony, carried by Ionic columns. The facade, in a mellow red brick with stone dressings, showed four arched windows and a matching doorway at ground level, with five magnificently tall windows above. It was these that lit the main hall.

Lavishly panelled in oak, with Corinthian columns and cornice rising to a height of 17 ft, the main hall measured 44 ft by 36 ft and was 24 ft high. On the side opposite the five windows was a 'musician's gallery', supported on columns and approached by two staircases. Beneath the gallery was a fireplace, with a chimney-piece of Pavonassa marble and an oak overmantel, richly carved in the manner of Grinling Gibbons, with flowers and cupid's heads. The doorways at each end of the hall were ennobled with columns and pediments, and the folding doors themselves were pierced and carved in the grand manner with instruments picked out in gold leaf. Over each door was a carved panel on which musical instruments and flowers ran riot. The room was lit by two large, silvered chandeliers, each carrying twenty-four electric lights. The entire effect was magnificent and awe-inspiring. Customers, tiptoeing across a broad carpet spread over the polished oak floor, scarcely dared to mention anything so sordid as money to the assistants, resplendent in their morning-coats.

Indeed, the very entrance was calculated to inspire at the outset a proper respect for music. Modelled on the staircase at Ashburnham House, Westminster, it was panelled in plaster to represent painted wood. At the top, a double screen of Ionic columns opened on to an ante-room which was to house Roubiliac's 1738 statue of Handel that had once graced Vauxhall Gardens and which Henry Littleton had purchased in 1880 for Westwood House.

But once past the grandeur, Novello's was laid out with a keen eye to practicality. Behind the main hall was a suite of rooms, including a board room heavily reminiscent of Westwood House; while beyond the hall was a 'club room', intended, we are told, 'for the use of any who may visit the establishment, either to look over music, to meet private or business friends, to send a telephone message, write letters, etc...a convenient rendezvous, especially for visitors from the country'.[16] On the next floor were stock rooms, rooms for editors, rooms for *The Musical Times* and *School Music Review*, while above that was a floor devoted to general and publishing offices, and the wholesale and postal side of the business.

It was all very practical, though curiously upside down. The ground floor windows on to Wardour Street were, at this stage, earmarked for subletting as shops. They were occupied by various firms, including the Imperial Ottoman Tobacco Regie, until 1928 long after Novello's had begun to wish they could have the extra space for themselves.

Thus, four years short of its centenary, the firm that Vincent Novello had unwittingly founded settled itself with due magnificence in the Soho that had always been its home.

CHAPTER TEN

WARDOUR STREET

The years between the setting up of Novello's as a limited company and the end of World War I saw the greatest expansion in the catalogue that the firm was ever to know. The 1915 edition is laid out on the same lines as that of 1893, but it is more than double the size. The number of new publications is staggering. New works appear in every category, and new categories have been created. The impression is one of buoyant optimism for the future of British music, and an almost reckless enthusiasm for promoting its welfare.

Perhaps the most important of the new sections is that devoted to music for schools. This already amounts to some fifty pages and includes examples of everything from action songs to operetta. Behind all this activity stands the figure of Dr William McNaught, editor of *The School Music Review*, a magazine tailored to the needs of music teachers that Novello's began to publish in 1892. Each issue (a mere 1½d) contained 'one or more School Songs, in both notations, suited to the capacities of the children in the different divisions of schools, which may [also] be purchased separately'.[1] These, together with articles of general interest to teachers, reports of school concerts, reviews of new music and so forth, were nicely calculated to stimulate an interest and lead the satisfied customer to further explorations of the catalogue.

One new section which would undoubtedly have been of special interest was that devoted to Cecil Sharp's arrangements of folk and country dance tunes, with historical notes and descriptions of the steps involved. There are three main collections: *The Morris Book*, and *The Country Dance Book*, both published in five parts (at 2s 6d each, and 3s 6d when bound in cloth), and a three-part collection called *The Sword Dances of Northern England*. Again it seems that the Novello ear was very much in tune with the times.

Even in those sections of the catalogue that might be expected to be most conservative there are surprises. In church music there are now two pages devoted to anthems and services in Welsh. Later, Novello's were to print hymn books in Gaelic, Afrikaans, Zulu and Hebrew. But it is the choral and orchestral sections that contain the most significant additions. In the ninety–one pages these sections occupy are the names of nearly all the composers who were caught up in the great reawakening of British musical creativity. And having so long nurtured a belief in British music, it was perhaps only fitting that Novello's should be rewarded with the discovery that among those names was one of genius and international significance: Edward Elgar, the greatest English composer since Purcell.

In alphabetical order, these are the composers that Novello's were prepared to encourage during this period, often to the extent of printing lavish full scores: Granville Bantock, William Bell, Rutland Boughton, Frederick Bridge, Samuel Coleridge-Taylor, Frederick Corder, Frederic Cowen, Walford Davies, Thomas Dunhill, Edward Elgar, Balfour Gardiner, Edward German, Josef Holbrooke, Gustav von Holst (as he was before the war), Hamish MacCunn, Alexander Mackenzie, Hubert Parry, Ethel Smyth, Arthur Somervell, John Stainer, Charles Stanford and Arthur Sullivan. The list is supplemented by a string of names that have now lost all significance, either because they were primarily organists forced into composition by the circumstances of their post–as were Herbert Brewer, Charles H. Lloyd and Charles Lee Williams by their Three Choirs connections; or because they served a fashion that is now dead–as did Alfred R. Gaul, Henry Gadsby and J. H. Maunder (whose *Olivet to Calvary* is still sometimes performed).

Leaving aside Elgar's masterpieces, all of which were published by Novello, the choral works that still remain alive are Coleridge-Taylor's *Scenes from the Song of Hiawatha* (in particular the opening section, *Hiawatha's Wedding Feast*), Parry's *Blest Pair of Sirens* and Stanford's cantata *The Revenge*. This may seem a very small quantity of cream to be skimmed from a very great quantity of milk, but it is probably about average in terms of music that dies in, or survives from, any period. What has to be remembered is that almost everything Novello's published in this line enjoyed a considerable popularity at the time. A glance through back numbers of *The Musical Times* will show how frequent and widespread were performances of works that are now no longer heard. Sullivan's ambitious oratorio *The Golden Legend* is a prime example; so also are Cowen's cantatas, and Mackenzie's. It may even be that there is life among these pieces yet–awaiting a change of taste and a caring hand to revive them. Recent exhumations of Parry's music certainly suggest that this may be true.

Among the established choral 'classics' in the 1915 catalogue it is interesting to note a marked increase in the number of Bach cantatas: thirty-seven, against eleven in 1893. Berlioz is also better represented, with *The Childhood of Christ*, *The Damnation of Faust*, *La mort d'Ophélie* and the *Te Deum* joining the *Grande messe des morts* and *Les nuits d'été* of the earlier catalogue. The main Brahms additions are the Requiem and the *Alto Rhapsody*, Novello's having failed to tempt him to write a full-blown oratorio comparable to *Elijah* in 1876, despite offers of £600 for the rights. There is also more of Purcell's music, including *King Arthur* and *Dioclesian*.

In some respects the British additions to the orchestral catalogue are the most impressive aspect of Novello's progressive policy. Not only were native composers now more fluent in this field, but opportunities for performance had markedly increased. In addition to Elgar's unique contribution, we find such works as Bantock's *Fifine at the Fair*, *Sapphic Poem* and *The Witch of Atlas*, Coleridge-Taylor's Ballades in A minor and D minor, Cowen's overture *The Butterfly's Ball*, the four *English Dances*, and Fourth and Fifth symphonies, Balfour Gardiner's *Overture to a Comedy*, Edward German's symphonic poem *Hamlet*, *Symphonic Suite*, First and Second symphonies and *Welsh Rhapsody*, Hamilton Harty's *With the Wild Geese* and Josef Holbrooke's symphonic poem *Byron*. Then come Parry's Symphonic Variations, *Overture to an Unwritten Tragedy*, *Lady Radnor's Suite*, and Second, Third and Fourth symphonies, Sullivan's Symphony in E (the 'Irish') published posthumously, and Stanford's 'Irish' Symphony (a great success both in this country and abroad) and Symphony no. 4. Altogether, fifty-two British composers are represented, with some 168 works–100 of which were engraved in full score.

As with the contents of the choral catalogue, only a handful of these works has kept any kind of place in the repertory, and then, with the exception of Elgar's masterpieces, only sporadically. But it is a list which contains much that ought not to be forgotten. Indeed, occasional revivals and recordings of such pieces as Hamilton Harty's *With the Wild Geese*, Bantock's *Sapphic Poem*, and, above all, the symphonies of Sullivan, Stanford, and Parry, all confirm that Elgar was not the only British composer who could handle an orchestra and the symphonic method, even if he was by far the greatest.

Little was added to the chamber music catalogue during this period, apart from J. B. McEwen's Quartet in A minor, Thomas Dunhill's Piano Quartet in B minor, and a number of Cobbett-inspired *Phantasie* quartets by Frank Bridge, James Friskin, William Hurlstone, H. Waldo Warner and Haydn Wood. The most interesting additions to violin music are contained in the series edited by Alfred Moffat under the title 'Old English Violin Music'. This includes sonatas by William Babell, John Collett, William Croft, Henry Eccles, John Humphries, James Lates and John Stanley. Contemporary composers, however, are poorly represented, with sonatas by Walford Davies (no. 1 in E minor), and J. B. McEwen (Piano Sonata in E minor), as the only substantial works—though solitary excursions by Cyril Scott, *An English Waltz*, John Ireland, *Bagatelle* and John Foulds (*Variazioni ed improvvisati su un tema originale*) are intriguing. In the organ catalogue, now much extended, Parry's Seven Choral Preludes stand out, and John West's edition of 'Old English Organ Music' must have made a welcome change from the very Victorian bias of earlier catalogues. Guilmant's Symphony op. 42 and Widor's Third Symphony are prominent among the organ display pieces.

There are also outstanding and adventurous additions to the list of 'musical literature'. Stainer's pioneer *Dufay and His Contemporaries*, and *Early Bodleian Music*, Sir George Grove's *Beethoven, and his Nine Symphonies* and Lafontaine's *The King's Musick: A transcription of Records relating to Music and Musicians (1460–1700)* are all works of scholarly importance which must have been undertaken at the time with very little prospect of financial gain.

Not all Novello publications, however, were actually originated by the firm. Many were obtained by the wise purchase of plates and copyrights as they came up for sale at the dissolution or reorganization of rival publishers. This was a practice the firm had always followed: not only improving their catalogue in the process, but ensuring a perhaps longer life and wider publicity for the works they took under their wing. Sometimes the purchase served to complete a series they carried already, as for example, the acquisition of Volumes 1 and 2 of Parry's *English Lyrics* in December 1899 at the sale of Stanley Lucas, Weber, Pitt and Hatzfield, Ltd. The thirty-eight plates and their copyrights were bought in for £19 and joined Volumes 3 and 4 that Novello were already publishing (the whole splendid series eventually reached twelve volumes, the last two being published posthumously).

Certain other publications were undertaken as 'author's property'. In such circumstances the composer paid for all the costs of printing and production, leaving Novello's to stock and advertise the material and pay him something in the order of a third of the retail price on all copies sold. This practice was particularly rampant between about 1880 and 1930, and continued, discreetly and on an ever-dwindling scale until about 1950, when it was dropped altogether. By 1970 all the music published in this way had been handed back to the composers or their heirs.

Inevitably, author's property publications led to the firm lending its name to a great deal of rubbish—one thinks, for example, of F. Reginald Statham's monumentally inept cantata *Vasco da Gama*, which appeared in 1895 and promptly sank without a trace, and the multitude of hymn tunes, anthems and services apparently being manufactured in every vicarage and organ-loft in the kingdom. But it was also under this scheme that Alfred R. Gaul's best-selling cantatas first saw the light of print, and when the opportunity arose, in March 1920, the firm was very happy to purchase his copyrights for a reasonable £1600. Nor did they make a mistake. One of those copyrights, *The Holy City*, which had first been performed at the Birmingham Festival of 1882 and had sold 162,000 copies by the time of Gaul's death in 1913, went on to have an active life of nearly 100 years before finally going out of print in 1978. Even so reputable a composer as Sir Walford Davies published his music in this way, while men with rich patrons delighted in the scheme: Lord Howard de Walden underwrote lavish editions of several of Josef Holbrooke's works, including his ambitious operatic trilogy *The Children of Don, Dylan* and *Bronwen*. And if the firm's reputation suffered, they were certainly not alone among publishers in operating such a service—how else would Mrs Mark H. Judges' intriguing *Meditation in Canterbury Cathedral on the Announcement of the Death of Archbishop Benson* have come before the public? At least it could be argued that the practice kept the printers in business: an important point in the difficult days after World War I, and when they were paid by the number of notes they engraved or set up in type.

The firm's choice of composers and works seems to have been guided almost entirely by the tastes and instincts of its music advisers (John West being the main authority at this period), for the directors were businessmen rather than musicians. Alfred Henry Littleton had undergone some degree of musical training and was a man of considerable culture: his collection of early printed music, including examples from Wynkyn de Worde to the beginning of the eighteenth century, deeply impressed visitors to the International Musical Congress of 1911 (largely organized by the firm), and his house in Lancaster Gate boasted several fine portraits of composers, including Handel by Denner, Arne by Zoffany and Purcell by (?) Kneller. It is, however, doubtful if his musical sensibilities went really deep; he was head of an important publishing house and ran it efficiently, but he would probably have been just as happy in any other money-making sphere. He expressed an occasional preference for a particular composer—the music, or personality of Sir Alexander Mackenzie seems to have pleased him—but beyond that he does not appear to have exerted any obvious artistic influence.

Augustus Littleton was, if anything, even less of a musician. His preference was for the theatre. He took a great delight in amateur theatricals, and hobnobbed famously with Sir Henry Irving. In a lordly, distant sort of way he kept an eye on the printing side of the business, but seems to have entertained few very positive thoughts about its artistic policies. On the strength of the firm's prestige, however, both brothers were elected to distinguished offices in music: Alfred becoming Master of the Musicians' Company (1910–11), and Augustus President of the Livery Club of the Worshipful Company of Musicians, 1922. Both served on the committee of the Royal Choral Society, and Alfred on the Council of the Royal College of Music. Both were in a position to pull strings for their favourite composers, and both, discreetly, did so.

Fortunately the firm was served by a number of perceptive musicians, including, from 1890 to 1908, August Johannes Jaeger (1860–1909), Elgar's beloved 'Nimrod'. As a lengthy obituary in the *Spectator* put it:

The services that Jaeger rendered to many of the British composers of today cannot be easily over-estimated. For these services were not confined to a liberal interpretation of his official duties and responsibilities as the representative of a great publishing house. He was an indefatigable propagandist and proselytiser. All that he wrote and said was animated by a heartfelt sincerity, and the only thing that disappointed him in his friends was when they failed to share his enthusiasms. His attitude was not judicial. Music either left him cold or filled him with ecstasy. But he always contended that the newcomer should have the benefit of the doubt until he was self-condemned.[2]

Had it not been for Jaeger's particular enthusiasm for Elgar, Novello's might easily have lost him to another publisher. Though his relations with the Littletons were cordial enough, there were moments of strong disagreement, even to the point (1899) of complete breakdown. But Jaeger was there to help mend the breach, soothing and encouraging Elgar's touchy genius, and Novello's went on to publish most of his major works.

Jaeger's faith in Elgar, and Littleton's acquiescence in it, nevertheless had to surmount numerous trials. Despite the success of his early choral works and the *Enigma Variations*, there were moments when it looked as if he might prove to be a liability. The initial failure of *The Dream of Gerontius* is a case in point, and it took many years before any return was seen on the cost of printing *The Apostles* and *The Kingdom*. Yet Novello's continued to issue his scores in lavishly engraved editions. The full scores (which include the oratorios) were particularly magnificent and such as few present-day composers could hope for.

Even financially Novello's were, in the end, reasonably generous and helpful to Elgar. Though they never paid him the extravagant sums they doled out to Gounod (for in the short term he never sold like Gounod), they were not mean. For *Gerontius* he argued successfully for a down-payment of £200, a royalty of 4d on each copy of the vocal score (after printing expenses had been cleared), and 10 per cent on each item issued as a separate number, the orchestral *Prelude*, for example, and 'The Angel's Farewell'. For *The Apostles* he was able to hold out for £1000, paid in four instalments spread over 1903–09, with a royalty on the vocal score after 10,000 copies had been sold (it was in fact to sell an average of 450 copies a year, as against 2350 of *Gerontius*). Moreover, the firm was particularly attentive in securing him lucrative conducting engagements when the bills of his rather grand lifestyle could not be met from his earnings as a composer. All in all, Novello's treated their greatest composer reasonably well, and began to reap their full reward only some thirty years after his death.

In the meantime there were any number of best-selling works that could finance the risks taken on Elgar and his contemporaries. They ranged from editions of the classics (*Messiah* was issued in a new and somewhat more scholarly edition by Ebenezer Prout in 1902), to such works as happened to catch the public's fancy for a short while. There was also the matter of outside printing.

This had been carried on since the earliest Dean Street days. For having set up as his own printer, J. Alfred Novello soon found that the needs of his publishing house were insufficient to keep his printers busy. The move to Hollen Street only emphasized the disparity, and Novello's accordingly began to broaden their activities as outside printers. The work they were eventually able to undertake included an extraordinary variety of publications: everything from Bibles to war-time ration books, the rapid weekly printing of forms for Cope's football pools, and the regular monthly order of 250,000 copies of whatever Foyle's Book Club had in mind.

Part of their success was almost certainly owing to a wise decision taken in 1935 to register the printworks as an entirely separate company, under the name of the Hollen Street Press. This move, it was correctly anticipated, would enable the firm to get print orders from publishers who might not wish to have the musically-associated name of Novello on the work. And though Novello's would have been reluctant to admit as much, it also helped to erase the memory of certain anti-trade union practices—in particular an ill-advised action that had occurred earlier in the century.

This had come about as the result of a strike among the music compositors in January 1911, who had asked for their hours to be reduced from fifty to forty-eight a week. The board rejected the claim and settled the matter by recruiting non-union labour, and reorganizing the works so as to cut the staff from 140 to 128 hands. At first it seemed a matter for congratulation—had not the weekly wage bill been reduced to £190? Only gradually was it realized that trade unions had long memories.

Further rumblings occurred in the years immediately after World War I. Some of them even affected the normally docile office staff. In October 1919, for example, Wardour Street presented what the directors termed, somewhat apocalyptically, a 'manifesto' demanding a revision of wages. Augustus Littleton declared that he 'did not feel vindictive' (though clearly he was very put out), but thought that the time had now come to 'put the Company's house in order'.[3] Nothing much was done, however, and in the following year the rumblings grew more intense. Minutes for the board meeting of 27 April 1920 record the directors' fears that they would shortly be brought 'face to face with Trades Unionism in some form or other'.[4] To offset this dire fate they suggested that the employees be steered towards the Printing Trades Alliance and away from the more aggressive National Union of Printing and Paper Workers which, they declared, was 'dominated by a man of the most objectionable Bolshevist type!'.[5] In the event, revolution was not to stalk the pavements of Wardour Street.

Similar flurries of indignation ruffled the board's stately calm when, in 1927, the staff suggested they might be allowed the benefits of a superannuation scheme. The directors were upset. Had it not been 'the practice of the Firm for many years to grant pensions on retirement of Members of the Staff on account of sickness, old-age, or incapacity of any kind, on a much higher scale than [was] usually adopted by most firms?'.[6] But it was also true that the directors enjoyed their patriarchal status. Being generous afforded an agreeable sensation not to be compared with the formal obligations of a superannuation scheme. In the end they gave way, and in 1933 a pension scheme was set up. At the same time they also gave way on the matter of trade unions–for it had now become clear that if they did not give in, valuable print orders would be lost.

In all these matters Novello employees were not dealing with a specially reactionary board of directors, but merely with one that was very old-fashioned and weighed down by the success of its nineteenth-century heritage. One small but very typical example of their gentle-manly innocence is recorded in the minutes of 24 January 1911, when the firm was faced with its first factory strike. The chairman on that occasion was Augustus Littleton, who solemnly reported that he had 'nearly succeeded in persuading the Music Compositors, but had [had] to leave to catch a train at the critical moment'.[7] Nobody seems to have thought his order of priorities left anything to be desired.

Whereas the Novello family had been lucky with Alfred remaining unmarried and therefore being obliged to pass on his firm to a man of proven ability, the Littletons spawned heirs and in-laws and were consequently touched by dynastic ambition. Under the Deed of Settlement made in 1887 it was laid down that each director had the right to nominate a son to enter the business and continue as his successor. That right soon became an obligation. Littletons followed Littletons, and Brookes followed Brookes. Only the Gills faded out of the picture by failing to supply the necessary male heir.

As a recipe for maintaining the health of a business, which depended, by its very nature, on imagination and speculative foresight, it was not good. The wonder is that the inheritors proved to be as able as they did! Fortunately they had the support of an amazingly loyal and long-suffering staff, endlessly prepared, it seems, to keep things going and save them from themselves.

CHAPTER ELEVEN

LITTLETONS AND BROOKES

The complicated process of sharing out the ownership of Novello & Company, Ltd among the firstborn of the original directors began in October 1905 when Henry John Littleton (Alfred's son) and Walter Littleton (Augustus's) reached an age when they might be allotted the necessary shares and therefore qualify for seats on the board. Henry John Littleton, however, died in 1914, the same year as his father, but his brother, Alfred Joseph Brooke Littleton (usually known as Jack Littleton) qualified in the same year, thus continuing the direct line. Henry Brooke's sons, Charles and Harold, became directors in 1916 and 1919 respectively, and there for a while matters rested. There were no further additions until 1953, when Jack Littleton's son John, and Walter's son Henry assumed their share of the, by now, rather broad mantle. The network widened again in 1957 when Charles Avenell, Walter Littleton's son-in-law, became a director. Two more Brookes joined the firm, Charles's son Peter, in 1939 and again after a period of war service, and Harold's son Henry in 1961, but neither became directors.

In defence of the family merry-go-round it is perhaps only fair to point out that directors were also brought in from outside: men who had earned their place by their proven value to the firm. These included the works manager Harold Hanhart (1934), Dr Adolf Aber (1937) and Harold Veyzey Strong, recruited in 1942 after his own company, Henderson & Spalding, had suffered under wartime bombs. Strong's son Laurence was appointed in 1955, Lewis S. Baker, the company secretary, in 1958, Eldon A. Ffitch, manager of the printing works, in 1960, and Walter Emery, the Bach scholar and music adviser to the firm, in 1964. These additions brought qualities to the board that could not be guaranteed by the laws of inheritance, and were therefore of vital importance to the welfare of the firm.

Musically, the most outstanding of those required to follow in paternal footsteps was Harold Littleton Brooke (1880–1956). He had studied at the Leipzig Conservatorium (1899–1902) under Teichmüller, and had then joined the editorial department of Novello's. Later he worked with Jaeger in the publishing office. Eventually he came not only to direct the firm's publishing policy, but also to take a very active part in preparing manuscripts for publication. He had exactly the qualities needed in a music editor–being both scholarly and practical. Sir Arthur Bliss was only one of many composers who remembered his advice with gratitude:

I have learnt a great deal from him as to how music should actually *look* on paper. His object was always to simplify. He tried many ways, for instance, of making difficult cross–rhythms look easier and more natural in print. The layout must never appear more complex than absolutely necessary. He had a quick eye for mistakes in manuscript, and I was always aware of his critical attitude to the music itself. He would suddenly rap out, "I can't understand what *that* has to do with this passage", or "You will never get altos to take *that* leap in tune." I had an admiring respect for his judgment on music of mine that he knew almost as well as I did, and as a result I have often used the blue pencil in time, and to advantage.[1]

Elgar too seems to have felt a similar respect for his advice, and certainly regarded him as friend as much as publisher.

He was also an excellent choral conductor and for several years directed the Harold Brooke Choir–a small band of select voices that gave concerts at the Bishopsgate Institute. This had developed out of the so-called Novello Choir that William McNaught had recruited from the firm's staff, and their friends, in about 1905. Harold Brooke became its conductor in 1913, and again in 1918 after a wartime break. It was a large choir (about a hundred voices) and delighted in performing such works as *Hiawatha's Wedding Feast*, and Parry's *Pied Piper* (as at the Central Hall, Westminster, in June 1920) but it could not be very selective in its membership. Eventually, in 1924, it was disbanded only to be revived in the following year on a much smaller scale (thirty-six voices) and a highly selective basis. In this guise it gave excellent concerts over the next five years, often reviving the lesser known works of Bach and Handel in meticulously authentic editions. Something of its quality can be gauged from the fact that Bliss wrote his delightful *Pastoral: 'Lie strewn the White Flocks'* especially for the Harold Brooke Choir and dedicated it to them.

Even so, Harold Brooke had his limitations, and Bliss, in his appreciation, was specific about them: 'He was a man with definite blind spots where modern music was concerned, and it was no use trying to convince him when he sat listening to it, bored or irritated'.[2] One of those 'blind spots' was Vaughan Williams; another, Benjamin Britten, both of whom were snapped up by rival publishers.

In consequence, the new additions to the catalogue between the wars were somewhat conservative. There are some surprises—Holst's great Choral Symphony (1925) and masterly *Egdon Heath* (1922), for example, and his operas *The Perfect Fool* and *At the Boar's Head*. None of them was calculated to make money (though the ballet music from *The Perfect Fool* unexpectedly proved to be a popular concert item). Much more typical is music by Sir Granville Bantock, Sir Walford Davies, Sir George Dyson, Sir Arthur Bliss, Herbert Howells and E. J. Moeran.

It was perhaps inevitable that Novello's should sport a conservative image. The great house in Wardour Street, the immense catalogue of choral classics, the chaste, familiar brown covers in which each vocal score was bound (the work of the Dalziel Brothers, high priests of Victorian design), all spoke rousingly of the nineteenth century and tradition. Did they not publish the music of three Masters of the King's (and Queen's) Musick: Sir Edward Elgar, Sir Walford Davies and Sir Arthur Bliss? Were they not entrusted with the printing and publication of the *Form and Order of Service for the Coronation* of four successive sovereigns: King Edward VII (1902), King George V (1911), King George VI (1937) and Queen Elizabeth II (1953)—each volume a masterpiece of the printer's art? Novello's had become so deeply associated in the public mind with everything established and traditional in British music that it had become easy to forget the pioneering courage that had made the firm great, and even easier to discount it as a force for the future.

Again, it has to be said that some of the blame lay in the manner in which the board of directors had been recruited, and the very complacent way in which individual members conducted themselves. In May 1928, for example, the minutes tell us that the board had begun to consider the possibility of employing a general manager 'who would be bound to keep office hours. Directors were free to come and go as they pleased, [and] were not as a rule suitable for Manager's posts'.[3] This caused consternation among the Brookes, who, being less heavily endowed with shares in the firm, were more dependent on a definite salary, and prided themselves on their attention to duty. Harold Brooke felt obliged to point out that 'the work and enterprise of the so-called Junior Directors, who were no longer young (being all in the neighbourhood of fifty years of age) had long been cramped by the fact that in everything they did they were expected to consult with and obtain approval of the Senior Directors'.[4] And if this was true for directors, it was doubly true for the staff that worked under them. Attitudes had changed very much for the worse since the days when nineteen-year-olds had been given their heads in the running of the business.

In view of the somewhat uneasy relationship between certain members of the board—largely a matter of Littletons versus Brookes—it is not surprising that when an entirely new element arrived on the scene it would have no difficulty in establishing a firm foothold. That new element was Dr Adolf Aber.

Aber (1893–1960) first appeared in March 1936. He was a man of considerable musical eminence. He had been director of the Institute for Musicology at Berlin University, and the first music critic on the prestigious *Leipziger neueste Nachrichten*. In 1927 he had become a partner in the Leipzig music-publishing firm of Friedrich Hofmeister, and it was in this capacity that he approached Novello's with 'proposals about certain sole agencies he had acquired'.[5]

The thought of agencies 'which must extend our foreign sales very considerably if taken up'[6] enchanted the board. A letter was despatched to Dr Aber: 'We understand you intend to reside principally in England and that you will give us the exclusive benefits of your advice and experience, and will do everything in your power to make this department a success'.[7] He was, in short, welcomed with open arms. But it does not seem to have occurred to anybody that Dr Aber, correctly diagnosing the prospects for Jews in Nazi Germany, was busily creating a job for himself in a more hospitable climate.

Nevertheless he was a brilliant man, with much to offer any music publisher. He came along with a perfectly valid set of proposals which, at a time of falling home sales, must have seemed very attractive–even if hindsight suggests that the firm might have been better occupied in lending a sympathetic ear to the more adventurous British music of the time.

And he was as good as his word. Agencies followed in quick succession: Robert Forberg, Wilhelm Zimmermann, Ernst Eulenberg and G. Alsbach & Co. in 1936; Anton J. Benjamin and Hinrichsen in 1937; Peters Editions, F. E. C. Leuckart and Editions Maurice Senart in 1938. Each brought a sense of international enterprise to a hitherto resolutely British firm–and each was about to be invalidated in the approaching war.

There can be no doubt that Dr Aber's schemes were excellent, in their way. But there can also be no doubt that he was able to run rings round the board. He attended his first meeting as director on 4 October 1937, and offered up a 'Memorandum of the Reorganisation of the Publishing Business', which was immediately adopted as a basis for future action.

It was probably this preoccupation with continental efficiency that led Novello's to abandon, in 1937, their American outlet through the New York firm of H. W. Gray & Company. The history of this connection, however, is a curious one. The proprietor of the American firm was Willard Gray, who had joined Novello's as an employee in 1882. He proved to be a bright young man, and in 1892 was appointed manager of the firm's branch on East 17th Street. New York and the spirit of American enterprise proved far too attractive, and he promptly set about building up a company of his own. By 1906 Novello's were so disenchanted that they sold out entirely to their former employee, but retained his services as agent for their publications. But even this did not prove very satisfactory–the directors' minutes record numerous heart-searchings on the matter. A firm decision to abandon their connection was finally reached in February 1937.

In any case, the directors had other things to worry about. In December 1937 negotiations began for the purchase of the Arlington Works and its associated land at Twickenham, which was to be used as warehousing now that the lease on a building at Great Titchfield Street was about to run out. Wardour Street, completely occupied from ground floor to roof, was already too small to house the vast stock of music that had to be carried, let alone the great piles of outside printing of all shapes and sizes. And in May 1939 negotiations began with Messrs Page & Thomas (Chesham) with an eye to an eventual take-over and a further expansion of outside printing facilities.

There were domestic problems too. In March 1938 Hiawatha Coleridge-Taylor brought an action against the firm in which he claimed that it was no longer entitled to a copyright in his father's cantata *A Tale of Old Japan*. He based his argument on the fact that the process of signing the original contract had straddled the period of the passing of the Copyright Act of 1911 and its coming into force as law. Even though it was clear, from letters, that an agreement had been entered into before the act came into force on 1 July 1912, the judge ruled against Novello's. A Court of Appeal thought differently, however, and the judgment was very properly overturned.

Indeed, the Coleridge-Taylor family had been a frequent source of embarrassment since the composer's death in 1912. They found it hard to accept that he had sold the copyright of *Hiawatha* outright for a mere fifteen guineas, and had then had to watch it develop into an enormous financial success. Letters of protest were written to *The Times* in 1912 and 1913, Sir Charles Stanford joining in with particularly snide comments which suggest that he was busily grinding a personal axe. Novello's pointed out that they had made certain ex gratia payments, including the sum of £100 to enable the composer's impoverished widow to complete the purchase of her house, but the matter still rankled. It turned up again in 1921 when, in response to further letters of complaint from Mrs Coleridge-Taylor the board 'absolutely declined to create Royalties on works which belonged to the Company (outright)',[8] but in the same breath (presumably feeling a trifle guilty at all the profits *Hiawatha* continued to make!) sent her a cheque for £300, to be delivered 'without any explanation'.[9] A further veiled protest in June 1925, by way of a letter to *The Times*, brought no response: Novello's evidently deciding that enough was enough and that they were not to be pilloried merely for having struck a profitable but perfectly legitimate piece of business.

As things stood, it was just as well there were profits to be made from certain works. In the years immediately following World War I, and on through the 1920s and the 1930s, music publishing, like every other business, found itself in difficulties. Prices which had increased slightly in January 1918, rose again in April 1919. Penny numbers, which had become 1½d, remained the same, as did everything up to one shilling. But 1s 4d items rose to 1s 6d, with 6s 6d items to 7s 6d and 12s 6d items to 15s. Further substantial increases followed in July 1920, bringing prices in the middle range to double what they had been before the war. Although these were reduced somewhat in July 1923, it was clear that the old days of 'cheap music' were fast fading away. And if it now seems ludicrous that there was still music to be purchased for 1½d and 2d, it must be remembered that a young man such as Eldon Ffitch could enter the firm's employment in March 1924 as a junior clerk at a salary of £1 a week, less national insurance.

This was also a period of change in music-publishing methods, and not all the new ideas were welcomed by the board. For example, at the beginning of 1926 the matter of the embryo Performing Right Society had to be considered. Novello's were very dubious. Surely the collecting of such fees would frighten off the choral societies on whom they depended for their bread-and-butter? By joining the scheme, publishers would surely forfeit some of the control they held over actual right of performance? It was not until December 1936 that they could bring themselves to sign a contract and at last fall into line with every other British publisher.

The various upheavals recorded in the directors' minutes, as Novello's reluctantly began to grapple with the problems of the twentieth century, make amusing reading. In November 1929, for instance, there was much concern over their travellers' apparent inability to increase sales. The remedy seemed to lie in the creation of a special 'pushing department'–the more sonorous word 'Promotion' not yet having been coined. Earlier (October 1920) there had been the problems arising from 'the want of accommodation and control of the staff's feeding habits'.[10] The chairman was distressed by the sight of 'continual tea-making, even at 10 o'clock in the morning by the girls whose day did not commence until 9 o'clock, and the habit of cooking or warming up substantial meals on a gas ring...'.[11] It was all very alarming, and not at all like the old days. The matter was debated, but the meeting came to no very definite conclusion and then, as usual, adjourned for an early lunch.

Wartime brought its own special problems. Wardour Street was closed for a week, in order to make proper provisions against air-raids and so on. The staff was technically dismissed, but offered re-engagement on new terms. These were at first intended to include a reduction of all salaries by one third, later amended to one fifth. This only lasted until the end of the year, when it was discovered that the business had not collapsed and that such draconian measures were unnecessary.

In the meantime publication continued. *The Musical Times* for November 1939 went out of its way to reassure its readers that, come what may, Novello & Company, Ltd would continue to serve music. Substantial scores by Dyson, Bliss and Moeran had been issued in the months immediately before hostilities commenced, and more were now promised: Dyson's Symphony in G, Bliss's Piano Concerto, organ music by Herbert Howells and reprints of the Peters Edition for which the firm still acted as agents.

Even doubts raised in certain quarters about the ethics of 'trading with the enemy'[12] were satisfactorily quelled (*The Musical Times*, February 1941), Novello's pointing out that to ban the performance of German copyrights would be to lose music by Dvořák, Sibelius, Grieg and a dozen others—including even Elgar! Royalties from such copyrights had in any case to be paid to the custodian of Enemy Property for ultimate disposal.

Yet it was precisely matters of this kind that were to involve the firm in the most embarrassing event in its entire history. There had been warning rumbles in 1939 when Lengnick & Company laid claim to the hire fees of certain works owned by Anton J. Benjamin of Leipzig, with whom Novello's supposed they enjoyed an exclusive agency— quite unaware that the Nazis had forced the firm into a change of ownership. The matter was settled amicably enough. But in 1945 the more serious disagreement arose over the ownership of several Hinrichsen copyrights.

Novello's, it will be remembered, had acquired an agency with Hinrichsen in 1937. In December the following year Dr Henri Hinrichsen had been forced to assign his business to two Nazi-approved gentlemen. When the matter came to court, early in 1951, it was ruled that confiscatory legislation of this kind could have no effect in British law, and that the copyrights involved belonged solely to the Hinrichsen family. This, in effect, meant Mr Max Hinrichsen, who had found refuge in England—his father and his brother perished in concentration camps.

The whole business could probably have been settled without re-course to law. Novello's, acting on Dr Aber's advice, had been singu-larly helpful to Max Hinrichsen, and by keeping many pieces from Hinrichsen's Peters Edition in print, virtually guaranteed that he could start up in business again in the country that had offered him shelter. Unfortunately there were conflicts of personality. Not everyone in the firm liked Max Hinrichsen, so when in 1945 he announced that he intended to print certain lucrative works (including Sinding's *Rustle of Spring*) in which Novello's believed they held the agency, legal action was taken to restrain him, and this, in due course, led to full-scale court proceedings to decide who actually owned what.

In spite of the fact that Novello's had negotiated their agreements in good faith, they were at fault in not recognizing the essentially illegal manner in which Hinrichsen's had been deprived of their firm. Had they understood this they would surely have been prepared to waive their claim to copyrights which, however valuable, had only a few years to run. Instead, they chose to demand their pound of flesh–and promptly and deservedly lost the action. Max Hinrichsen was award-ed compensation of £8000, Novello's forfeited their interest in a number of important copyrights and were ordered to pay costs, which on a nineteen-day court hearing were considerable.

Altogether, the years immediately after World War II were not kind to Novello & Company, Ltd. Serious negotiations with Richard Strauss, with a view to obtaining the copyrights in his symphonic poems, broke down in April 1947 when the directors refused to increase their option from £1000 to £3000–a magnificent example of short-sighted penny-pinching. A business partnership between Novello's and Hofmeister proposed by Dr Aber in 1950 eventually came into existence under the name of the Musik-Union. It lasted, fitfully, for a couple of years, but proved very unsatisfactory. When it was eventually wound up in 1957, Novello's were grateful enough to retrieve the money they had originally invested. A glance at other firms' catalogues told them that they had not backed the real winners among the up-and-coming British composers. And over everything hung the knowledge that the Wardour Street lease would not go on for ever, and that their present way of life was something of a fool's paradise.

CHAPTER TWELVE

TO THE PRESENT DAY

One of the most striking things about the Novello catalogue is the fact that it was preserved almost intact until well after World War II. Certain pieces were allowed to go out of print, but there was seldom any need to abandon slow-selling stock simply to make room for new publications. The public grew accustomed to being able to ask for almost anything, and was therefore deeply shocked when post-war conditions forced the company to undertake much harsher disciplines.

During the inter-war years publishing policy did not differ much from the pattern set up in the nineteenth century. New anthems and services were added in profusion, giving an outlet to dozens of ephemeral talents and a few of more lasting worth—the church music of William H. Harris and Herbert Howells is particularly notable. Part-songs, too, appeared with monotonous regularity: useful material for choirs and competitions, but not all aspiring to the quality of E. J. Moeran's *Songs of Springtime*. New works for chorus and orchestra were also much in demand, and some that were published proved to be of permanent value: Sir Arthur Bliss's *Pastoral* (1929) and choral symphony *Morning Heroes* (1930), and Holst's First Choral Symphony (1925) are among them, with perhaps a thought to be spared for Dyson's ambitious *Nebuchadnezzar* (1935) and *Quo vadis* (1939). Herbert Howells's magnificent *Hymnus paradisi* also belongs to this period, though it had to wait until 1950 before being released for performance and publication. Indeed, the market for these, and similar works by lesser men (such as the ever-practical Eric Thiman), showed little sign of declining, and as late as 1959 the firm still found it worthwhile to purchase the remaining years of certain Maunder copyrights.

Yet it was on the orchestral side of music publishing, thanks to the growing importance of performing-right fees, that the future lay. And in spite of having failed to lay claim to Vaughan Williams, William Walton and the young Benjamin Britten, Novello's could boast an interesting range of composers. Sir Arthur Bliss's concertos for cello, violin and piano, his ballets *A Miracle in the Gorbals, Adam Zero* and *Checkmate*, his music for the film *Things to Come* and his magnificent *Music for Strings* would have graced any catalogue–as would E. J. Moeran's Symphony in G minor, Sinfonietta, Serenade in G, and concertos for cello and violin. Hamilton Harty's two concertos (violin and piano) were also works of considerable quality, and there was much to admire in Sir Granville Bantock's large output. It has been something of a misfortune that British reluctance to enthuse over more than one or two native composers at a time has allowed such names as these to drift into neglect and misunderstanding.

Though several moves were made in the early part of the century to expand the Novello catalogue by purchasing those of other companies (Donajowski's, for example, was on the market in September 1911 at £11,000, while Augener's was seriously considered in 1909 at £65,000), nothing concrete was done for fifty years. And then, in May 1959, the Edwin Arnold catalogue was purchased for £4250, to be followed by that of William Elkin & Company at £5500. Both were absorbed into the main catalogue, though the Elkin additions were allowed to maintain a separate identity. In this way a number of minor Elgar works were brought into the fold, as well as a quantity of interesting pieces of Cyril Scott, William Baines and Roger Quilter.

The mood of quiet expansion also touched the actual Novello premises. Various rearrangements of the work space took place in Wardour Street, and in 1945 a factory was acquired at Slough (313–14 Farnham Road) for photo litho book and colour reproduction. By 1948 Novello & Company, Ltd were equipped with some of the finest printing machinery in the country.

By 1955, however, the eventual expiry of the Wardour Street leases began to loom very large indeed. It was quite clear that Novello's, or any other music publisher for that matter, would not be able to afford to renew them at modern rates. What they were currently paying–a mere £1000 a year—was derisory. The increase would be tremendous and insupportable. A drastic change was required.

The first thought was to expand the factory at Chesham, and in 1957 adjoining land was purchased with this in view. In June 1961 the premises at Twickenham were sold for a sum that would finance the proposed new buildings. But a month or so later, a printing firm, H. C. Dunckley (Wrotham), Limited, came on the market and the board decided that these premises would offer a much more convenient solution to the problem. Accordingly, £60,000 was spent on purchasing the Dunckley shares, and an option taken on purchasing the land, the factory and fourteen dwelling houses at Borough Green.

In the following year the first offers began to come through for the remainder of the lease on Wardour Street. Negotiations were not completed until 1964, when £214,000 was paid by a property developer. Roubiliac's statue of Handel went to the Victoria and Albert Museum for £10,000—a sum which surprised everybody, for its benevolent presence at the top of the stairs had long been taken for granted.

By 31 March 1965 Novello & Company, Ltd had re-established themselves. The editorial offices and showroom were still in Soho, at 27 Soho Square, a few yards away from the original premises in Frith Street, but the administrative offices, warehouse and printing works were now in Kent, at Borough Green. All attempts to 'develop' the Wardour Street site failed, and Pearson's masterpiece is now, appropriately, inhabited by the British Library and honoured as a 'listed' building.

Saddening as these changes seemed to many, they were in fact a blessing in disguise, for they forced the firm to face the economic facts of post-war life. To survive, Novello's would have to become altogether slimmer and trimmer. It was now no longer possible to carry such a large stock. Room could always be found for such valuable items as the various *Messiah* editions, which had by now sold in millions, but slow-moving pieces would simply have to be let go out of print—some indeed would have to be deliberately withdrawn.

At the same time it was decided to abandon a large part of the very considerable outside-printing services that had grown up over the years. This may not have been a wholly wise decision, for the factories at Slough and Chesham were singularly well-equipped and in a good position to hold their own in a competitive market. But the family members of the board were not really interested. The property, equipment and shares of Page & Thomas were sold in April 1966 for just over £140,000, and the Slough works in October for £35,000–substantial, but not wholly realistic prices. By the end of the year Novello's had reduced themselves to the kind of size and commitments the board felt able to cope with and were preparing to do battle with the realities of twentieth-century publishing. They had every reason to be on their mettle, for in 1963 they had received a tremendous shock.

On 5 June the board heard, to its utter astonishment, that the company was in imminent danger of being taken over, lock, stock and printing machines. It seemed that cash offers had been made to various shareholders by a certain indemnity trust on behalf of a gentleman whose sole interest would be to sell off the firm's assets (such as the leaseholds) and then dispose of its catalogue to another publisher. Novello's as Novello's would cease to exist, and the gentleman concerned would pocket a quick and handsome profit. Worse still, it became clear that it was one of their number–doubtless irritated beyond endurance by the board's hopelessly old-fashioned ways–who had helped to engineer the situation. Only a prompt closing of ranks could prevent disaster. The board acted, and saved the day.

But if such a thing could happen once, it could happen again. The prospect of asset-stripping attracted a great many sharks, and Novello's, with their widely dispersed shares, must have seemed a very tasty and easy victim. Over the next few years a number of serious attempts were made to gain control, and it became increasingly obvious that the situation could only be stabilized if a major British company could be found to purchase all the shares and be content to run the firm as a going concern.

The answer did not come until 1970. And then, auspiciously on 23 April, an agreement was reached with Lord Bernstein's Granada Group for the purchase of all the shares at a valuation of £540,000. The offer (£35 for each £10 ordinary share and £5 for each preference share) had been taken up by the shareholders–some opting for cash, others preferring Granada shares in exchange.

Externally, the most obvious and immediate change was the removal of the London editorial offices and showroom to premises owned by Granada at the corner of Beak Street and Upper James Street, off Golden Square. Internally, the changes began to make themselves felt only gradually. They were largely concerned with improving efficiency: tightening up on the very indulgent way of doing business that almost invariably creeps into old-established family firms. Without demanding that it should in any way neglect its duty to music as an art, Granada made it clear that Novello's was in the business of selling a commodity and that certain consequences must follow.

The most generally alarming of these involved abandoning a great many pieces of music that had been many years in print, but which sold only in small quantities. The decision was a hard one: it upset customers, who had long grown accustomed to being able to buy copies of the most obscure items at a moment's notice; it upset composers, who by now had assumed a god-given right to the manifold services their publisher afforded and seldom stopped to consider if their works were an economic proposition.

However, it did not mean that music with a poor sales record was lost forever. Many pieces were simply withdrawn into the hire library in sufficient quantities to satisfy any performances that might be called for. Others were whittled down to reference copies, which formed the material for a Uniprint service whereby customers could ask for photo-copies to be made in the quantity they required. All this meant that expensive storage space could be devoted to those works that sold in reasonable quantity and earned their keep. Fortunately there were still a great many of them. What Granada had acquired was a very considerable property. Not perhaps as grand and all-powerful as it once had been, but still very sturdy and, more important still, full of potential.

The process of reawakening had begun immediately after World War II. Guided partly by Harold Brooke, partly by the services of its music advisers (including H. A. Chambers and Reginald Jacques), and partly by the enterprise of its publishing managers Harry Fowle, who retired in 1969, and Basil Ramsey, who left in 1975 to form his own company, Novello's had sought and found a remarkably varied number of young British composers. The list of those born in the twentieth century, and whose works Novello's were to publish in any quantity, is very impressive. It includes Alan Bush, Benjamin Frankel and Eric Thiman (born in the 1900–1910 period); Geoffrey Bush, Joseph Horovitz, Michael Hurd, Wilfred Josephs, John Joubert, Kenneth Leighton, Bruce Montgomery, Anthony Milner, (1920–30); Peter Dickinson, Jonathan Harvey, Bryan Kelly, John McCabe, Christopher Steel, and Charles Camilleri (1930–40); Barry Guy and Nicola LeFanu (1940–50).

With the appointment of George Rizza in 1972, the company, after an interval of some sixteen years, was headed once more by a musician managing director. Rizza himself holds sole responsibility for Novello's publishing policy and also directs the activities of an increasingly important promotion department which is mainly concerned with fostering the professional performance of music by living composers.

Since 1972, he has published or acquired works by Thea Musgrave and Gerard Schurmann (born in the 1920–30 period); Richard Rodney Bennett, David Blake and Justin Connolly (1930–40); Martin Dalby, Roger Marsh, Giles Swayne and Michael Blake Watkins (1940–50); Stephen Oliver and Judith Weir (after 1950). An interest in foreign-born composers has also been maintained through the publication of music by Irwin Bazelon and Bernard Herrmann (USA), Naresh Sohal (India) and, more recently, Aulis Sallinen (Finland).

Though the bias is still towards perhaps relatively conservative composers whose music is of service to the public at large and not merely the fad of an avant-garde minority, the wide range of styles on offer remains considerable and provides a desirable cross-section of British music.

Nor were all of Novello's new publications quite as solemn and 'respectable' as its older customers had come to expect. In 1963, for example, schools were startled, and then delighted, by a new genre– the 'pop' cantata. The first of these, by Herbert Chappell, was a setting of Vachell Lindsay's famous poem *The Daniel Jazz*. It was published not without some misgivings on the part of the older members of Novello's staff, but rapidly became a best-seller. Successors soon followed: Michael Hurd's *Jonah-man Jazz*, *Swingin' Samson*, *Hip Hip Horatio*, *Rooster Rag* and *Pilgrim*; *Captain Noah and his Floating Zoo* by Michael Flanders and Joseph Horovitz; Chris Hazell's *Holy Moses!* and *Joseph and the Amazing Technicolor Dreamcoat* by Tim Rice and Andrew Lloyd-Webber. By 1980 over a million and a quarter copies had been printed and the cantatas were being performed worldwide.

In purchasing Novello & Company, Ltd, Granada had also acquired a series of subsidiary catalogues. One of the most important of these was that of W. Paxton & Company, Ltd, whose main asset was the famous and extensive hire library formerly owned by Messrs Goodwin & Tabb. This had been bought in 1971 and was to turn Novello's into one of the country's leading sources of hired music.

Then there was the matter of Fairfield Music: a subsidiary established by Novello's in 1966 largely to exploit the film music of

Bernard Herrmann and handle certain types of music that did not fit the image of the main catalogue. In addition, Novello's were agents for a number of important German publishers, including Hänssler Verlag (Stuttgart), G. Henle Verlag (Munich), Musikverlag C. F. Kahnt (Wasserburg), Kistner & Siegel (Porz-Westhoven), Musikverlag F. E. C. Leuckart (Munich), Möseler Verlag (Wolfenbüttel), Willy Müller Suddeutschermusikverlag (Heidelberg) and Musikverlag Wilhelm Zimmermann (Munich). They also represented the American Wind Band Catalogue, Rubank, and were later to act as UK distributors for G. Ricordi Ltd (1979).

Another acquisition was the Lorna Group of publishing companies (1970), which dealt mainly with recorded pop music, while in June 1968, a new company was formed in the USA, Novello Publications Inc, in order to develop the parent firm's share of the market there. Later on, its offices and warehouse were established at Dobbs Ferry, New York.

Granada policy has always been to let its subsidiaries operate with the minimum of interference. Novello & Company, Ltd is still very much in control of its own destiny, and, since it regularly turns in a healthy profit, there seems to be no reason why this state of affairs should not continue. Its present staff—a mere 114, and a far cry from the old days when the printers alone outnumbered them—are headed by Sir Denis Forman, as chairman on Granada's behalf, with George Rizza as managing director.

CHAPTER THIRTEEN

NOVELLO MAGAZINES

During their 170 years Novello's have been responsible for a number of magazines devoted to various aspects of music and the arts. The most important of them, *The Musical Times*, is the main subject of this chapter, but there are others that have come and gone: some lasting only a short while, others for a respectable period that enabled them to make a significant mark.

The first Novello magazine venture was *The Musical World*, the prototype in all but size and shape of *The Musical Times*. It was launched by J. Alfred Novello in January 1836, with Charles Cowden Clarke as its editor. Despite its subtitle 'A Weekly Record of Musical Science, Literature, and Intelligence', several pages of each number were devoted to advertising the latest Novello publications.

Each issue contained sixteen pages, measuring 7¼ inches by 4¾, neatly printed by C. Richards of 100 St Martin's Lane and bound in mulberry-coloured paper covers. Publication took place 'every Friday afternoon at five o'clock'[1] at what was then a fairly stiff price, 3d. The hand of the Cowden Clarkes is apparent in the lines from *The Taming of the Shrew* printed immediately below the title:

> To know the cause why music was ordained;
> Was it not to refresh the mind of man,
> After his studies or his usual pain?
> Then give me leave to read philosophy,
> And, while I pause, serve in your harmony.

The contents of the first number set the pattern for the series. First an article of general interest: 'A Sketch of the State of Music in England from the year 1778 up to the Present' by Samuel Wesley. Subsequent issues were to match this with: 'Characteristics of Beethoven' by Henry J. Gauntlett; 'On the Objects of Musical Study' by Edward Hodges, Mus. Doc.; 'Instrumental Music' by George Hogarth; and so on.

The second item in the first issue is a general article on 'National Music' which seems to betray the tastes, if not the literary style, of Vincent Novello. This is followed by several pages of reviews: two on concerts (all in London), one on London opera productions and one on 'New Music'. The critical style is distinctly snappy. For example, we are told of a Mr Winter, appearing with the Italian Opera at the King's Theatre, that his talent

> is limited; the quality of his voice (a second, if not third-rate tenor) thin and unsatisfactory; and, as an actor, he deserves no consideration at all: he is the most un-mortified of passionate lovers, and the least varied as an attitudinarian—ending almost every sentence with pointing out behind him.[2]

Just over two pages are devoted to general musical gossip, past and present, under the appropriate heading 'miscellaneous'. Here we learn that Mendelssohn 'is putting the last touch to his sacred Oratorio of *The Conversion of St Paul*', that Meyerbeer's new opera *Les Huguenots* has 'met with great success' (though one would not think it from the singularly foolish remarks quoted from the Paris Correspondent of *The Times*), that Beethoven rescinded the dedication of the *Sinfonia Eroica* to Napoleon ('Shocking old radical! No wonder he died poor', is the editor's comment), and that the eight-year-old Mozart amazed London, according to the Hon. Daines Barrington, whose *Miscellanies* are extensively quoted.

There follows the poetry of a song by Charles Cowden Clarke, 'I love the talking of the giddy breeze', set to music (though as yet unpublished) by Felix Mendelssohn Bertholdi (sic). And last of all come the advertisements, mostly for new and recently published music—though later issues were to urge the unrivalled qualities of 'Thorn's "Potted Yarmouth Bloaters" and "Tally-Ho Sauce" (for fish, game, steaks, chops, cutlets, made dishes, and all general purposes)'.[3]

J. Alfred Novello sold *The Musical World* to the organ builder

Frederick Davison (partner in Messrs Gray and Davison) at the end of 1837, possibly because Charles Cowden Clarke's success as a lecturer left him insufficient time to run the magazine effectively. Editor then followed editor in fairly quick succession: Dr Henry Gauntlett, Henry Smart, George Macfarren 'senior'; and it was not until the critic J. W. Davison took charge in 1843 that any real sense of direction was achieved. Thereafter the magazine flourished and was, in fact, the only serious rival to *The Musical Times*. In 1854 it passed into the ownership of Thomas Boosey, and, considerably enlarged both in number of pages and overall size, continued until 1891.

During the last quarter of the nineteenth century Novello's launched two unsuccessful magazines, both apparently aimed at a readership slightly up-market of *The Musical Times*. The first appeared on 1 May 1875 under the title *Concordia: A Weekly Journal of Music and the Sister Arts*. It was to be published every Saturday, price 4d. The editor was the music critic and librettist Joseph Bennett, and the initial prospectus intimated that 'while holding definite options, [the magazine would] strive to make itself the organ of an enlightened eclecticism'.[4] There were to be articles on music, together with 'the sister Arts of Poetry, and Painting, the Drama, etc'. These were to be contributed by 'able writers', and among those promised were Joseph Barnby, William Chappell, W. H. Cummings, Edward Dannreuther, H. Sutherland Edwards, the Revd Henry Haweis, John Hullah, George Alexander Macfarren, Ebenezer Prout, Edward Rimbault, Charles Salaman and Dr John Stainer. 'On all matters involving criticism, *Concordia* will speak with a single desire that truth may be known; strong in the conviction that the temperate utterance of honest opinions must surely win respect.'[5]

What it failed to win, however, was a sufficient readership. Advertisements on its behalf appear in *The Musical Times* until March 1876, and then there is silence. The last issue was published in April.

The Musical Review, which began to appear on Saturday 6 January 1883, was even more of a disaster, lasting only six months. Its intention was to be 'a comprehensive weekly record of the progress of Musical Art in all its branches', based in London, because London was now 'one of the musical centres of the world', but concerning itself with developments thoughout the civilized world.[6]

The forthright and somewhat grandiloquent claims made on its behalf suggest the pen of Joseph Bennett, though no actual editor is named:

In furthering the interests of Art and Artists for the sake of Art alone, in combining due reverence for the classical models with ready appreciation of all that is hopeful and truthful in modern music, *The Musical Review* will endeavour to follow the example of Schumann's *Neue Zeitschrift für Musik*. Like that model of periodical literature, it will also endeavour to attract the interests of cultured amateurs, no less than that of professors, by avoiding abstruseness of treatment as far as a thorough discussion of the subject will allow...

The tone of the new journal may best be indicated by the proverbial saying 'Fortiter in re, suaviter in modo.' The unflinching truth will be spoken, but in no instance will personal susceptibilities be hurt without need. Only in the repression of incompetence and arrogant mediocrity will it be thought necessary to have recourse to the severer modes of criticism.[7]

But it seems that there was to be no market for the truth, however unflinching. Readers, professional and amateur alike, preferred to remain loyal to the homelier pages of *The Musical Times*.

Much more successful was *The School Music Review*, edited by Dr William McNaught and first published on 1 June 1892. Like *The Musical Times*, this was a monthly magazine which, in addition to articles of general interest, offered free music supplements. At 1½d it was a bargain that teachers could not ignore. Its aims, as set out in the prospectus, were very specific:

The establishment of a Journal specially devoted to the interests of Music in School is believed to be called for by the conspicuous development of the systematic teaching of singing and music generally that has taken place in schools during recent years.

Singing by note is now taught in upwards of 20,000 elementary and middle-class schools in the United Kingdom. As most of the music teaching is committed to the care of the ordinary school staff, the tuning of the ear, preservation of the voice, and the musical culture of the nation may be said to depend in a great measure upon the skill and training of the 120,000 teachers composing our educational army. It will be one of the first aims of *The School Music Review* to deal plainly with the questions of *what to do and how to do it* that constantly arise in connection with the varied musical needs of both teachers and pupils.[8]

Included in the first number were articles on 'The History of Music in Primary Schools', and 'On the Training of Pupil Teachers in Music', a series of 'Reports of School Entertainments' and three pieces of music (a hymn by Stainer, a 'Kindergarten Song' by Alfred Moffat and a 'vocal trio' by Franz Abt) printed in notation and in tonic sol-fa, extra copies of which could be purchased for 1½d.

Once again the formula of providing helpful information, taking notice of and reporting upon what the customers were themselves doing, and giving away specimen pieces of music proved attractive. A satisfactorily large readership was soon built up–each teacher a potential customer of Novello's rapidly growing school music catalogue.

William McNaught remained editor of *The School Music Review* until the end of June 1922. He was succeeded by Miss Mabel Chamberlain, who had been his assistant for many years. By this time, however, it was in financial trouble, apparently losing a steady £600 a year. Although sales figures rose under Miss Chamberlain's guidance, there still remained a deficit and in March 1930 the board of directors reluctantly decided the magazine must cease publication with the May issue.

For a while (July 1930 to January 1937) a brief information sheet, *The School Music Record*, was published at irregular intervals, but in November 1936 it was decided to try again, this time with a magazine entitled *Music in Schools* and with Miss May Sarson as editor. The first number appeared in March 1937, and continued each month until September 1940 when, largely in response to wartime economies, it became a bi-monthly publication.

The whole approach of *Music in Schools* was much more sophisticated, much less inclined to lay down the law on what to do and how to do it. It had been realized that music teaching was now more often in the hands of specialists. As if to underline this broader approach, the magazine changed its name to *Music in Education* with the May/June issue of 1944 and in this guise continued under the Novello wing until 1977, its last editors being William Elkin (1954–61) and Gordon Reynolds (appointed in September 1961). Though popular, the magazine's finances were variable and losses rather too frequent to be supported indefinitely. Macmillan's made a satisfactory offer in January 1977, ran it until December 1978 under the editorship of Paul Griffiths, and then closed it down altogether.

Novello's have also been concerned with two magazines they did not originate: *The Strad* and *Jazz Journal*. *The Strad* was founded in

May 1890 by Harry Lavender, proprietor of J. H. Lavender & Company, a small firm which specialized in the publication of string music and technical books, and Eugene Polonaski, who was its editor until 1892. Lavender became the sole proprietor in 1892 and remained so until his death in 1907. During this period, and until her own death in 1937, Mrs Emily Lavender appears to have acted as editor, assisted by a small team of specialists. Publication continued under her sons, Douglas and Eric Lavender, until Novello's purchased it in July 1964. It is now edited by Mr Eric Lavender, and the whole enterprise, having something of the nature of a trade magazine, has been singularly successful.

Rather less flourishing is the *Jazz Journal*, founded in 1948 by Sinclair Traill and acquired by Novello's in 1970. Recognizing that they were at something of a loss to know how best to develop a magazine that served the needs of a very different kind of music-lover from those they were accustomed to, Novello's eventually leased *Jazz Journal*, first to Billboard, Ltd (1977), and then to Pitman Periodicals (1979). It is currently edited by Burnett James.

The origins of Novello's most successful and influential magazine, *The Musical Times*, have already been touched upon and need be only briefly elaborated here. It began life in August 1841 as the *National Singing Circular*, a small news-sheet published at irregular intervals by Joseph Mainzer in order to advertise his 'System of Popular Musical Instruction'. This became Mainzer's *Musical Times and Singing Circular* in 1842; the first number was issued on 15 July, price 2d, and thereafter on a regular basis. It contained one general article, entitled 'Musical Education in England, in the Sixteenth and Nineteenth Centuries', a review of 'The London Musical Scene', two columns of miscellaneous musical news, brief reviews of two new pieces of music and a column of adverts. The remainder of the sixteen pages (some ten pages in all) was given over to a fairly detailed account of Mr Mainzer's peregrinations around Great Britain, and the universal success of his classes.

It was indeed success that led Mainzer to sell his magazine. A visit to Edinburgh in 1842, at the special request of the Lord Provost, proved a triumph and Mainzer thereupon offered himself as a candidate for the Chair of Music at the university. He was not elected, but the warmth of his Scottish reception encouraged him to turn all his attentions to that region. J. Alfred Novello took over the magazine in May 1844 (together with the agency for Mainzer's many musical and instructional publications) and brought out his first issue on 1 June.

Though smaller and relatively more expensive than Mainzer's original (1½d for eight pages), *The Musical Times*, as it was now called, presented a much smarter and more authoritative appearance than it did in his day. The type-face was clearer, the paper of better quality and the layout altogether more elegant. The change of name was also an improvement, though the legend 'Singing-Class Circular' was retained in small print.

In the first Novello issue three pages are given over to music ('In these Delightful Pleasant Groves' by Purcell), two to announcements of Novello publications, one and a half to a 'Brief Chronicle' of musical events and gossip, a half page to 'New Publications' (all from Novello) and one to an editorial reviewing the gratifying improvement in amateur music-making over the years.

What J. Alfred Novello had on offer was unashamedly a house magazine, as firmly dedicated to the advertisement of Novello publications as Mainzer's had been to the promotion of his methods. In the initial stages the great attraction must have been the musical supplement bound in as part of the magazine. Individual members of a choral society, or a group of friends who liked to sing together, could purchase the magazine and each month have an attractive piece of music, neatly printed and nicely calculated to stretch and satisfy modest talents. Mainzer had inserted pages of music in his own magazine, but they were nearly always by Mainzer, or aimed at the Mainzer method. Novello's were offering the readers real music by real composers.

J. Alfred Novello himself seems to have acted at the magazine's first editor until 1863, save for a brief period (1853–6) when his sister, Mary Cowden Clarke, took over. But he must also have had the cooperation of Charles Cowden Clarke and Edward Holmes (Vincent Novello's friend and pupil). Holmes (1797–1859), author of an exemplary *Life of Mozart* (1845) and *A Ramble among the Musicians of Germany* (1828), contributed detailed analyses of Haydn and Mozart masses (Novello publications), an important 'Life of Purcell' (1847), articles on 'Cathedral Music and Composers' (1850), 'English Glee and Madrigal Composers' (1851) and 'Beethoven's Mass in C' (1858), all of which, together with similar pieces by other authors, helped to turn the magazine into an organ of general interest and valuable instruction both for the ordinary music-lover and the professional musician.

During Mrs Cowden Clarke's editorship *The Musical Times* took on a distinctly literary flavour, with regular articles by Leigh Hunt in his usual flowery and rather inconsequential style. It was during this period (1855–6) that Sabilla Novello's translation of Berlioz's *Soirées de l'orchestre* appeared. And for a brief period, July 1852 to October 1853, a column was set aside for the editor of *The Dramatic and Musical Review* which appears to have been absorbed by Novello's in 1852.

It was not until 1863, when Henry Charles Lunn became editor, that *The Musical Times* began to attract the services of all the British musical scholars of the day. By 1877, the year in which Henry Lunn retired in favour of Dr William Alexander Barrett, the articles had become almost recondite. Chrysander's 'Sketch of the History of Music Printing from the 15th to the 19th Centuries', for example, argues a considerable increase in the sophistication of the magazine's readership, and it was certainly a far cry from the day when it was thought desirable to run advertisements for such nostrums as 'Dr Lacock's Pulmonic Wafers'–guaranteed in 1845 to give 'instant relief, and a rapid cure of asthmas, consumption, coughs, colds, and all disorders of the breath and lungs'![9]

By 1877 *The Musical Times* had also undergone several changes in its appearance. It now cost 3d and contained forty-eight pages: having risen to twelve in February 1848, twenty in December 1853 and thirty-two in January 1868. While the cover, having resembled *The Times* (with a banner title and two columns of advertisements), suddenly, in February 1877, assumed a highly elaborate pattern in black on white–all flowers, urns, and cherubs: the work of the Dalziel Brothers.

With a steadily increasing readership (14,000 by December 1870), it rapidly became the most influential organ of its kind in Great Britain. It was crammed with information of all kinds, skilfully weighing the needs of the amateur against the claims of the professional. The articles were scholarly and authoritative, yet readable and entertaining.

Detailed reviews of new music became a regular feature after January 1868. When necessary, they could be very sharp indeed–as, for instance, the reaction to the first appearance of the oratorio *Ruth* by George Tolhurst (a composer who found a dubious immortality as the William MacGonagall of music):

It is always, with us, a matter of regret that untried composers should submit their works to critical judgment after, instead of before, publication. Were the latter method more generally pursued, an adverse opinion upon the merits of a composition from the lips of a known friend might save years of anxiety and disappointment; but once the work is published, and formally sent for review, what verdict detrimental to the hopes of the expectant composer–however tenderly worded–will ever be accepted as the genuine opinion of an unprejudiced judge? Many a young and deserving musician, who might as a teacher, or perhaps even as a performer, have held a good position in the profession, has been ruined by the unfortunate delusion that nature has intended him for a composer. This feeling having once gained possession of him, there is little hope of his stopping short of an Oratorio. The scriptures are ransacked for 'words': songs, duets, and choruses cut to the pattern of the great standard works are thrown together; and out comes a huge book, to haunt its unfortunate author for the rest of his life, and to crush all hope of his steady advancement in the more humble path which he might have pursued both with honour and profit. We know nothing of Mr Tolhurst, and should have been pleased to know nothing of his oratorio...How so crude a composition as *Ruth* could have been performed, applauded, and favourably commented upon– even as far off as Melbourne, where it first saw the light of day–is to us a marvel...[10]

Mr Tolhurst was not pleased and responded with a very characteristic letter.

Above all, there was the monthly musical supplement with sacred and secular pieces alternating, sometimes music of the masters, but more often a newly composed piece, eminently suitable for choirs up and down the land, and eagerly purchased by them. One need only think of the November 1877 supplement, William H. Cummings's adaptation of Mendelssohn's *Festgesang* tune to the words 'Hark, the Herald Angels sing', to understand the impact these pieces might have.

Some idea of the value *The Musical Times* had for its nineteenth-century readers can be seen in an article of reminiscences published in the Jubilee number (1 June 1894):

The literary matter, which, while unpretentious, opened up a new world to thousands of budding amateurs. Through this medium we began to make acquaintance with the great masters of music, to learn the opinions of cultivated minds, and to gain some idea of the musical activities on the stage of the world–advantages not easily obtainable from the columns of the local newspaper, or through casual perusal of a high-priced London daily. Perhaps the most useful feature of the journal at that time was the brief paragraphs recording the doings of musical societies and classes all the country over. Apart from the information they conveyed, and the means of estimating the comparative popularity of composers and their works, these paragraphs served to excite emulation and stimulate progress. It may appear a triviality in days of universal and indiscriminate publicity, but it is a fact that the chance of figuring in the *Musical Times* was sufficient to encourage a good deal of hard work at preparations for 'public display.'[11]

Various improvements were announced in the 1894 Jubilee number: an enlarged type for certain major articles, thicker paper of better quality, and each number 'to be issued cut open'. A permanent enlargement to seventy-two pages was also announced, with a separate musical supplement in addition to the usual musical pages, which would frequently bring the magazine up to eighty pages. The price was now 4d.

After these changes the size, appearance and content of the magazine remained fairly static, changing in a marked way only with the onset of World War I when the cover assumed a sober blue-grey or buff and dropped the Dalziel swags and garlands in favour of a simpler boxed title and advertisements. Size and price fluctuated somewhat, eventually settling at 6d in 1919.

During World War II there was a dramatic reduction in the magazine's size to thirty-two pages, accompanied by a rise in price (1941) to 9d. Editors, following William Barrett, were Edgar Jacques (1891–7), Frederick George Edwards (1897–1909), William George McNaught (1909–18) and Harvey Grace (1918–44). Contents, of course, reflect the times with new sections being brought in to review areas such as radio and gramophone music.

Since the end of World War II the changes have been more dramatic. A simple, plain blue cover, with a blue border line round the edges and a table of contents in the centre, served from January 1957 to June 1960, during which time the price rose from 1s to 2s. This was followed in July 1960 by a series of buff, green or red covers with a solid block title filling the top half and a table of contents beneath chosen, according to the editor, because 'the demure blue cover, though agreeable, was in danger of being eclipsed by the many brilliant-hued journals now on the bookstalls'.[12] And doubtless it was for the same reason that the present pictorial cover, in a different colour each month, was adopted in January 1963.

The sudden, and to many readers very irritating change in size that came abruptly in January 1980, sweeping away the familiar and distinctive octavo in favour of a wider, squarer format, seems to have been made for a similar reason–to compete with other magazines. By this time, however, a revolution had also been forced on the prices that Novello's were obliged to charge. From 1s they had crept to 1s 6d (January 1957), then by easy stages to 4s (September 1965), and on into the snares and delusions of decimal currency (20p, February 1971), until the present and doubtless temporary price of 65p (104 times the original 1½d!) was reached in January 1981.

No marked change of editorial policy came until 1961 with the appointment of Andrew Porter as editor (1961–7). The editors before that date had been William McNaught (1944–53), Martin Cooper (1953–7) and Harold Rutland (1957–60), with a brief interregnum by Arthur Jacobs during the first three months of 1953 following the sudden death of Hubert Foss who had been appointed to succeed McNaught. Finding that under their hands the magazine had become rather too parochial, Andrew Porter, and his successor the present editor Dr Stanley Sadie, determined to raise its status by adopting a more scholarly and international approach. Since then, the articles have become increasingly the province of the musicologist and music critic, and while the magazine has gained respect in the eyes of music scholars throughout the world, it has undoubtedly lost its hold on the sympathies of the older type of musical amateur. Significantly, the decision (also made by Andrew Porter) to commission musical supplements from more avant-garde composers did not serve to lead the amateur gently into the twentieth century, but merely added another reason for eventually abandoning supplements as a regular feature.

But to make these criticisms is merely to underline the fact that *The Musical Times* has always reflected the artistic temper of the day. The old style of magazine is probably no longer needed; amateur music-making can find very little foothold in the most advanced music of our time, and there are organs of musical information (such as records, radio and television) undreamed of by our grandfathers. What matters is that the magazine should serve legitimate needs to the best of its ability, and like everything connected with a major publishing house, look boldly to the future from its solid basis in the past.

CHAPTER FOURTEEN

PRINTING AND PUBLISHING

When J. Alfred Novello set up shop as his own printer, he issued his first scores by the process of music engraving. Within a very short time, however, he had turned to music type as a preferred alternative wherever long printing runs were contemplated, linking this with the process of making stereo plates for greater economy and durability. These two processes, with variations, remained part and parcel of the firm's practice until well into the twentieth century, and engraving is still used today. The only significant addition came with the use of lithography, and later photo-lithography, as a more convenient method of multiplying what the engraved plate and the movable type had already produced.

Whatever method is adopted for originating a page of printed music, the craftsman involved has a number of considerations over and above those that face the printer of books. Consider the page you are reading. The printer has had to ensure that each line is perfectly horizontal and begins and ends at exactly the same place in order to produce vertical margins. Each word must be suitably placed inside the line, so that the eye does not run one into another. Each letter in the word must be equally spaced from the next. And, it goes without saying, spelling and punctuation must be correct. These problems are few compared with those that face the originator of a printed musical score.

Music has to be read vertically as well as horizontally. The notes must not only be correct in themselves but also be correct in relation to each other. Each bar must be laid out in such a way that the sense of the music (in particular its rhythm) is immediately apparent to the eye. If words are involved, as in vocal music, the spacing of the notes must take into account the physical size of each word—a single-syllabled word sung to one note can be short or long: 'in', for example, as compared with 'breadth'. Space must be left for directions affecting the performance—dynamics, speeds, inflections and so forth. Moreover, convention, and musical commonsense, requires that each page contains a complete run of bars. It is not reasonable to have half a bar on one page and the remainder on the next. There are no hyphens in music! Nor is a half-empty page desirable, though the last page of a chapter does not have to be completely filled. In short, the page of music, however it is produced, must be carefully designed. Its layout is a matter of skill and art.

So far as engraving is concerned the business of layout is a matter for the foreman engraver. He assesses the requirements of the music in relation to the size of the page, taking into account the number of notes (and words) in each bar, and the general appearance each page should present. He then takes a soft metal plate, usually made of pewter, and marks out exactly where each stave, bar-line, note and word will appear—scratching his design with delicate pin-point marks, using a kind of shorthand that can be translated by his fellow engravers into conventional notation. The finished engraving is then carried out, using a selection of steel punches and graving tools.

Each punch resembles a steel pencil with a musical symbol raised at the pointed end. Each symbol corresponds to those aspects of musical notation that never vary—the note-heads, clefs, accidentals and so on. The engraver stamps these marks into the metal, lightly tapping the punch with a small hammer.

Gravers are used to cut those aspects of notation that vary—the stem of a note, the length of a beam, the curve of a phrase mark and so on. The graver is a short steel blade, mounted in a wooden handle that fits comfortably into the palm of the hand. The cutting edge of each graver is shaped according to the work it must do: a graver designed to cut slender note-stems is different in shape from one designed to cut the gently swelling curve of a phrase mark.

The engraver begins by cutting the staves with a five-point graver. He then punches in the words (if there are any) and the note heads. Stems, tails and other details come in their appropriate order until the plate is complete. Everything, however, is done backwards—from right to left, in mirror fashion. It takes about four hours to complete the average octavo plate.

In order to check its accuracy, a proof must be pulled. The plate is rolled in a special ink, usually green, which clings to the flat surface but does not dribble into the engraved lines. A sheet of paper is placed against this and the whole passed through a light press. The music emerges as a pattern of white lines on a dense green background. This is carefully examined by the music-readers, and then by the composer, and any mistakes are marked in–a dot missing from a note, say. To correct a mistake the engraver pinpoints the offending area, turns the plate over and lightly taps the metal back into place. After smoothing and burnishing the surface he makes his correction. There is, of course, a limit to the number of times the same spot can be adjusted

At this stage it would be possible to print off the music direct from the plate, using a different kind of ink that settles into the engraved cavities but which can be wiped off the general surface. The result will be black notation on white paper. The disadvantage of this direct method, which J. Alfred Novello must have used in the early days, is that sooner or later the soft metal plate will show signs of wear and will have to be re-engraved in order to preserve a sharp image. The solution, as we shall see, was to link the engraved plate to the process of lithography.

Nevertheless it has to be said that engraving produces the sharpest and most elegant kind of printed music. Everything about it is the result of a craftsman's eye. From first to last the page is *designed*, and can therefore have the kind of artistic beauty that only a master craftsman can create. Unfortunately it is a dying art. From the days when they could employ a dozen engravers working long hours, Novello's are now (1981) reduced to two. Indeed, there are only half a dozen such men in the country. New methods have taken their place, and will inexorably continue to do so. But the loss to music when the last engraver lays down his tools will be greater than anyone is at first likely to realize.

Although essentially a more cumbersome method of obtaining a page of music, the business of printing from movable type adopted by J. Alfred Novello in the late 1840s was made possible by the very considerable improvements at that time in the design and casting of music type. As can readily be imagined, the problems in creating a fount of type to cover the innumerable signs used in music (far more than the mere twenty-six letters of the alphabet and a handful of punctuation marks), not to mention the fact that these signs involve curves, verticals and acute angles that cut across the horizontal grid of a stave, are very considerable.

It is not practical to lay down the stave in one printing and then superimpose the notation on top, though such methods have been attempted. Each sign, or part of a sign, must embrace part of a stave, so that stave and sign can be fitted together to make a whole. The result is a complex jigsaw involving hundreds of different pieces. For example, Messrs P. M. Shanks & Sons' Gem Music Fount contains 464 characters, while their Diamond Fount has 487. It needs little imagination to recognize the skill and patience required to set up a page of music from such an assortment. Compositors developed a remarkable facility, but the normal page was still a full day's work.

Nor is it difficult to imagine the sheer bulk and weight involved in carrying a sufficiently large fount to cope with work on any reasonably commercial scale. The inventory made in 1898 of the contents of Novello's Dean Street premises is startling, even when allowance is made for the firm's habitual tendency never to throw anything away. The various music founts weigh in at 37,312 lbs—more than 16 tons, valued in those days at £9,658 16s 6d (though presumably having cost rather more to buy). To this can be added a further 69 tons of assorted letterpress type and some 150 tons of lithographic stone.

One of the problems endemic in the early design of music founts concerns the matter of hair-line cracks and other irregularities appearing on the printed page at those points where the various characters failed to fit together absolutely smoothly. Examples of this can be seen in the cheaper sorts of music printing of the time. The founts cast specially for Novello's seem to have largely overcome this difficulty, and a well-set page of their printing can appear almost as smooth and elegant as one taken from an engraved plate. This neatness was greatly enhanced when the process was backed up by the use of stereo plates.

The stereo plate came into existence primarily as a method of saving wear and tear on music type, which was bound to deteriorate with each printing—though less rapidly than the engraved plate. It also enabled the printer to make do with a smaller quantity of type. The idea was both simple and ingenious. When a page of music type had been set up, a cast was made, originally by pouring in a specially fine plaster of Paris, but later by means of papier mâché, applied as sheets of tissue and blotting paper, liberally spread with a special paste. The resulting mould was known as a 'flong'.

This matrix was then placed in a casting-box, into which was poured molten stereotype metal (an alloy of lead, tin and antimony). When this hardened it made a plate: identical with the original type forme, which could then be broken up ('distributed') and used again.

The stereo thus enabled the publisher to store away, in convenient and permanent form, all the music he was likely to reprint, without involving him in a vast outlay in founts of music type. Stereos could also be worked upon, so that irregularities could be smoothed away and a more perfect impression passed on to the printed page. At a later date it became the practice to harden the surface of the stereo by giving it a thin coating of nickel or copper, by means of electrolysis. The copper coat produced a better finish in the printing.

The Dean Street inventory shows Novello's carrying a stock of 91,869 stereos in octavo and quarto size, 48,002 in smaller sizes, together with 117,902 engraved plates and a mixture of 39,300 plates of 'work in hand'.

Stereos, like engraved plates and direct music type, were subject to wear and tear during the course of successive printings, for it must be remembered that printing implies pressure, and pressure will inevitably lead to the deterioration of surfaces. It is here that the use of lithography came in, first utilizing the heavy lithographic stones, and then, more satisfactorily, a thin metal plate.

Lithography was invented in 1796 by a Bavarian actor and dramatist, Alois Senefelder. He discovered that a particular kind of stone (Solnhofen stone) would absorb grease but not water. He therefore wrote on a polished stone surface with a greasy kind of ink, coated it with a mixture of water and gum arabic, and then rolled it with printer's ink. The ink adhered to the greasy writing, but not to the watery surface (the water, of course, would not settle on the grease). The water and the floating ink were then removed. When paper was applied to the stone it would take up the ink held by the greasy outlines of what had been written. The process of damping, inking and rolling was repeated for each copy, until the original greasy outline became too blurred for further use. There were, however, chemical ways of prolonging the firm outline.

Lithography could be linked both to engraving and music type by means of a transfer print: treating the plates with a greasy ink, running off a print on specially prepared transfer paper and then applying this to the lithographic stone. Music could also be written out by hand directly on to transfer paper.

There is some evidence that Novello's used hand-copied transfers, but only on a very limited scale. They relied mainly on transfers obtained from engraved and type-set plates. In 1898 they carried over 150 tons of lithographic stone—some 279 stones of different sizes, sixteen of which, so the inventory tells us, were broken. There were also four stones capable of yielding colour work as, for example, in printing pictorial covers.

Novello's continued to use flat-bed stone litho-machines until 1913, when they were replaced by direct rotary presses and zinc-plate lithography. In the zinc plate method the surface of the metal was 'grained': pitted with minute cavities by being agitated in a special trough filled with marbles (or ball bearings) and an abrasive sand. The graining, a noisy and lengthy process, was carried out on the premises—one reason, perhaps, for several 'complaints' lodged by Hollen Street neighbours.

Graining meant that the zinc plate would now hold a surface of water, settling like linked puddles in the tiny cavities. Thus it could be treated like a lithographic stone with the ink adhering to the greasy outlines of the music, but not to the watered surfaces. Unlike the stone, the zinc plate was light to handle and could be fitted to the cylinder of a rotary press which, of course, would operate more quickly and efficiently than the flat-bed machine. And unlike the stone, which had to be cleaned and ground to a fresh surface, the zinc plate could be stored intact and ready for further use at a later date. If it was thought necessary to clean it and start again, this too could be done by immersion in a weak acid and then repeating the graining process.

The rotary press method was further improved by the introduction of 'offset' machines. Here the impression was first transferred to a revolving rubber-clad cylinder, and then from this to the paper. By this method it was possible to print satisfactorily on the kind of matt-surfaced paper that musicians prefer (a hard, shiny paper is not easy to read from). Novello's installed offset machines in the 1930s.

From the evidence of the 1898 inventory it is possible to infer, more or less exactly, the kind of printing methods used by the firm in its early days. No fewer than twenty-two platen presses are listed, of various sizes and all hand-operated. The three earliest are a Crown Broadside Imperial Press by Cope & Sherwin, dated 1836, a Folio Albion Press by Hopkinson & Cope and a Platen Galley Proving Press by Essen, both dated 1844. It is presumably on these that J. Alfred

Novello began as a printer in his own right. Similar presses seem to have been acquired at regular intervals up to 1877, their platens ranging in size from 18 inches by 12, to 36 inches by 23. With one exception, a 'Columbian' press by Clymer, dated 1845, they were all 'Albion' presses.

The next stage, dating probably from the late 1860s, saw the introduction of four Wharfedale machines, and then, in the 1880s, six perfecting machines of various makes. The perfecting machines were a considerable advance, for on these it was possible to print both sides of a sheet in one continuous operation. Both types were power-operated, and the inventory lists three engines, one of ten and two of sixteen horsepower, together with a seemingly endless selection of shafts, pulleys and driving belts. Until the firm finally turned over to electricity, the Dean Street and Hollen Street premises were a cat's cradle of such devices–clanking and shuddering, and, in the days before rigid safety requirements, presenting an almost infinite number of dangers to the hapless operators.

With the move to the more spacious and custom-built factory in Hollen Street (Dean Street was merely a converted private house and the two factory-like upper floors added in the 1880s can still be seen), larger, faster and altogether more up-to-date equipment could be installed. From 1919, when Harold Hanhart took over as works manager, advances seem to have been made on all fronts. In 1928, for example, monotype composing machines (a type-casting machine operated from a keyboard) were introduced, and in 1933 the first Double Quad Letterpress Miehle Perfector. By the late 1930s, when the Hollen Street Press was accustomed to handling such orders as, say, the monthly 250,000 copies for Foyle's Book Club, it was possible, by using two machines, to print a 256-page novel in one operation–both perfecting machines printing 128 pages (sixty-four a side) at a stroke. This would then go immediately to the cutting and folding departments, and on to the binders.

The next major change of method came after World War II and involved the process known as photolithography. In this, the old idea of a greasy ink impression on litho stones or zinc plate was replaced by a photographic image. Grained zinc plates were still used, but their surfaces were coated with a light-sensitive film. Those areas of the film that were exposed to light would instantly harden and become permanent, while the unexposed parts would remain soluble and could be washed away by developing in water. It was therefore a simple matter to take a 'negative' from an engraved plate (white notes on a black background, derived in exactly the same way as the ordinary proof), place this over the sensitive plate and expose it to an intense light. The light passed through the white notation, hardened the film beneath and produced a reverse image. When the surrounding areas were washed away, the staves and notes would be left as a slightly raised image on the plate and could be treated by the normal lithographic process. It is this highly efficient method that is still in use today.

In recent years, however, considerable changes have been made in the way in which music reaches the 'negative' stage of the photo lithographic process. A proportion is still engraved; but this dying art is not likely to outlast the present century. Other methods of origination are available ranging from hand copying (by an expert copyist, or as a facsimile of the composer's own manuscript, if neat enough), and the musical type-writer, to the various 'nota set' methods of laying down musical symbols from transfers. But whatever the method, considerable skill is involved if the result is to be pleasing to the eye. Novello's still retain a small engraving staff, and have music type-writers on the premises, but other methods of origination are given to specialist firms as the need arises.

It should perhaps be mentioned that although the firm abandoned any large-scale use of music type in the 1930s, except for such items as hymn books where it was appropriate in the context of so much letterpress, they retained the services of one music compositor, Jack Taylor, until he retired, in his eighties. His task, in those latter days, was to set up music examples within the texts of such items as Royal Philharmonic Society programmes.

Whatever the method used for printing a piece of music, it is essential that the craftsmen involved should receive their 'copy' in a condition that makes it possible for them to carry out their task smoothly and efficiently. Though it might be supposed that manuscripts arrive from the composer in exactly this state, the reality is often rather different. A manuscript may be neat and legible, but it is unlikely to bear much resemblance to the 'house style' required by the publisher and expected by the public. The men who make sure that it is brought into line are the publisher's 'readers'. Their task is to check every detail: picking up any errors the composer may inadvertently have made (a not infrequent occurrence), rearranging the way he has set down his notation so that it is consistent and unambiguous, and sometimes even raising questions on points of musical practicability.

When proofs are ready, they must subject them to the closest scrutiny, noting and correcting every error before passing the proofs to the composer to be finally checked. Such men need to be highly trained musicians, and it has always been Novello's pride that their own staff is exceptionally skilled. Paradoxically, it is only when their work passes unnoticed that their contribution is greatest.

On the letterpress side of the business a considerable revolution was effected in 1978 when all the type-setting machinery was abandoned in favour of the computerized 'Edit-Writer' system. With equipment that takes up less than one sixth of the space and involves less than half the staff it is now possible to do the same amount of work in much less time. The text is typed on a keyboard and instantly appears on a small screen in front of the operator. It can be corrected at will, and the result is stored in a memory bank ready to be transferred, via photography, to one or other of seven offset-litho machines.

It is possible that music will eventually come to be originated in the same way. Such methods already exist, but they are still in their early stages and are very costly to operate (the patent-holders require a royalty on each job undertaken). Unfortunately the photographic setting of music is too small a field to attract the kind of investment and research needed to bring it to the same degree of efficiency and cost-effectiveness as has been possible with the printed word.

Now that the Hollen Street Press and Page & Thomas have been sold, the printing side of Novello & Company Ltd is devoted mainly to serving the needs of its publishing activities. A small amount of outside work is undertaken (about 15 per cent of the total), and a very high standard is still maintained, whether in elaborate colour printing or simple black and white. Case-binding is no longer done on the premises–gone are the days of elaborate tooling and riotous gilt lettering! A work-force of printers and binders that in its hey-day numbered over 400, is now slimmed down to thirty-four, with a team of eighty operating the publishing, hire department, despatch and general office side of the business. Computers reign where clerks once toiled.

New situations call for new solutions, though the problems, in a sense, remain the same. Novello's, once rather reluctant to countenance change, now seem to have taken the measure of the challenges that face all printers and publishers, and are as keenly equipped as any to meet them. What the future holds for music publishing is anybody's guess. But whatever it may be, it is certain that Novello & Company Ltd will be there to play their part.

A NOVELLO POSTSCRIPT

It is commonly assumed that the late Ivor Novello was in some way connected with the firm and the family. This, however, is not so. He was born David Ivor Davies, and recognizing that there was more mileage in 'Novello' as a professional name, he appropriated it from his mother, who had been christened Clara Novello Davies out of period admiration for the singer. Madame Clara Novello Davies, as she liked to style herself, was not a godchild of Clara Novello; but, like her son, merely someone who knew the publicity value of a good name.

MANUSCRIPT SOURCES
AND COLLECTIONS

There are two main collections of manuscript and printed material relating to the Novello family and firm: the contents of the private library and files of Novello & Company; and the 'Novello Cowden Clarke Collection', donated to the Brotherton Library at the University of Leeds by the Contessa Bona Gigliucci in 1953.

A brief account of the contents of the two main collections may be helpful:

The Private Library and Files of Novello & Company Ltd
These include a number of letters to and from the Novello and Littleton families, together with a large quantity of Vincent Novello's music manuscripts and transcriptions. Composers' letters and contracts dating from before about 1890 are poorly represented, but thereafter fairly fully. Stock books, inventories and documents relating to company affairs, including buildings and their contents, exist to cover the period 1898 onwards—including minutes of the board meetings. Before that date, the material is very sparse. The music files contain a comprehensive collection of publications, starting in 1811. There are a handful of photographs and portraits.

The Novello Cowden Clarke Collection
This important collection contains 975 volumes from the library of Charles and Mary Cowden Clarke, together with 450 letters to and from the various members of the Novello family and their friends.

Important letters from Vincent and Mary Novello, Leigh Hunt, Charles Dickens and Douglas Jerrold are included. There are also various documents referring to Alfred Novello's career, including the agreement with Henry Littleton for the sale of the firm. Giuseppe Novello's notebooks, various photographs and portraits, and the sketch-books of Edward Novello complete the collection.

Manuscript sources in private hands

These consist mainly of letters from various composers to Novello and Company, together with a handful of letters from various members of the Novello and Littleton families. They are not of outstanding interest, but some throw light on nineteenth-century publishing terms. Most are now the property of Henry S. P. Brooke, who preserved them when Novello's moved from Wardour Street.

BIBLIOGRAPHY

Altick, Richard, *The Cowden Clarkes*, Oxford, 1948
Bennett, Joseph, *A Short History of Cheap Music*, Novello, 1887
Cowden Clarke, Charles and Mary, *Recollections of Writers*, Low, 1878
Cowden Clarke, Mary, *The Life and Labours of Vincent Novello*, Novello, 1864
Cowden Clarke, Mary, *My Long Life*, T. Fisher Unwin, 1896
Gigliucci, Valeria, *Clara Novello's Reminiscences*, Arnold, 1910
Mackenzie-Grieve, Averil, *Clara Novello*, Bles, 1955
Medici, Nerina & Hughes, Rosemary, *A Mozart Pilgrimage*, Novello, 1955
Novello & Company, *The House of Novello*, Novello, c. 1938
Swinyard, Laurence (ed.), *A Century and a Half Years in Soho*, Novello, 1961

Major articles in *The Musical Times*

Littleton *v* Gounod   July 1873
A Novello Centenary   October 1881
A History of *The Musical Times*   January 1894
Our Jubilee   June 1894
Vincent Novello   September, October, December 1903
Soho and the House of Novello   December 1906
The Novello Centenary   June 1911
Henry Littleton   January 1923

NOTES

The following abbreviations have been used to indicate the main sources of information referred to in this book:

Novello—The private library and files of Novello & Co. Ltd
Leeds　　—The Novello–Cowden Clarke Collection, in the Brotherton Collection at Leeds University
Private　—Documents in private hands

CHAPTER ONE

1　Title page to Vincent Novello's first publication. Novello
2　Giuseppe Novello's notebooks. Leeds
3　*ibid.*
4　*The Life and Labours of Vincent Novello*, p. 2
5　*ibid.*, p. 2
6　*ibid.*, pp. 3–4
7　*ibid.*, p. 6
8　*ibid.*, pp. 61–2
9　Vincent Novello's will (16 March 1844). Leeds
10　Letter to Edward Rimbault, 24 July 1847. Novello
11　Letter to Mary Sabilla Novello, 28 January 1839. Leeds
12　*Recollections of Writers*, p. 220
13　*The Life & Letters of Charles Lamb* edited by T. N. Talfoord, 1857
14　*Recollections of Writers*, pp. 165–8
15　*My Long Life*, pp. 11–12

CHAPTER TWO

1　*The Song of Drop O'Wather* by Harry Wandsworth Shortfellow.

GeorgeRoutledge & Co. London, 1856, pp. 49–50

2 *The Diaries of William Macready, 1833–51*. London, 1912
3 *Clara Novello's Reminiscences*, p. 52
4 *ibid.*, p. 37
5 *Windsor and Eton Express*, 27 October 1832
6 Letter to Sir John Trevelyan, quoted in *Clara Novello*, by Averil Mackenzie-Grieve, p. 112
7 *ibid.*, p. 122
8 *ibid.*, p. 153
9 *Musical World*, 24 November 1860
10 *The Life and Labours of Vincent Novello*, pp. 9–10
11 *ibid.*, pp. 17–18
12 *My Long Life*, pp. 6–7, 13–14

CHAPTER THREE

1 Title page and prelims of Vincent Novello's first publication. Novello
2 *ibid.*
3 Title page, *The Evening Service*. Novello
4 *The Life and Labours of Vincent Novello*, p. 23
5 *ibid.*
6 *Recollections of Writers*, pp. 231–2
7 *Clara Novello's Reminiscences*, pp. 31–2
8 *The Letters of Charles Lamb*, ii, pp. 456–7
9 *Samuel Wesley, Musician* by James T. Lightwood. Epworth Press, 1937. Letter of 29 July 1816, p. 181
10 Mrs Vincent Novello, letter dated 12 October 1840. Leeds
11 *The Musical Times*, July 1844, p. 24
12 J. Alfred Novello's indentures. Leeds
13 J. Alfred Novello, letter dated 15 July 1848. Leeds
14 Mrs Vincent Novello, letter dated 12 October 1840. Leeds
15 J. A. Stumpff's subscription list, 24 June 1829. This forms part of Vincent Novello's travel notebook. Leeds
16 *The Life and Labours of Vincent Novello*, pp. 26–7
17 *ibid.*, p. 34
18 *The Infant's Prayer*. Novello
19 Mrs Vincent Novello, letter dated 29 April 1839. Leeds
20 Vincent Novello, letter dated 12 June 1845. Novello
21 Vincent Novello, letter dated 16 January 1849. Leeds
22 *A Legend of Florence*. Introductory note to Act 2
23 *ibid.*
24 Italy. Novello
25 Letter to the Working Classes of Great Britain. Leeds
26 *The Life and Labours of Vincent Novello*, p. 64

CHAPTER FOUR

1 Novello pamphlets. Novello, and also Leeds
2 *ibid.*
3 *The Musical Times*, October 1848, p. 1
4 *The Musical Times*, December 1906, p. 800
5 *Musical World*, 25 March 1836
6 *The Land without Music* by Bernarr Rainbow. Novello, 1967, p. 120
7 *The Musical Times*, June 1844, p. 1
8 *ibid.*, p. 2

CHAPTER FIVE

1 *The Musical Times*, January 1923, p. 17
2 *The Musical Times*, July 1846, p. 14
3 Novello
4 *A Short History of Cheap Music*, pp. 49–50
5 Process explained in Chapter 14
6 Novello pamphlets. Novello, and also Leeds
7 *The Musical Times*, May 1850, p. 324
8 *The Musical Times*, April 1855, Preface to vol. VI

CHAPTER SIX

1 *Morning Herald*, 18 June 1849
2 *The Musical Times*, April 1850, p. 299
3 *ibid.*, p. 298
4 *The Musical Times*, October 1855, p. 124
5 *ibid.*
6 *The Musical Times*, December 1850, p. 95
7 *ibid.*
8 *The Glee Hive*, i, preface
9 *ibid.*, ii, preface
10 *The Musical Times*, December 1850, p. 95
11 *The Musical Times*, December 1851, p. 308
12 *The Musical Times*, November 1853, p. 287
13 *ibid.*
14 *The Musical Times*, December 1852, p. 99.
15 *ibid.*
16 Queen Victoria's Diary, 13 May 1854
17 *The Cowden Clarkes*, p. 181
18 *Letters to an Enthusiast* by Mary Cowden Clarke (1902), pp. 300–01
19 Novello pamphlets. Novello, and also Leeds
20 *ibid.*
21 J. Alfred Novello, letter dated 1873. Leeds

CHAPTER SEVEN

1 Novello catalogue, April 1858. Novello
2 *ibid.*
3 *ibid.*
4 *ibid.*
5 *ibid.*
6 *ibid.*
7 Henry Littleton, letter dated 7 June 1867. Novello
8 *The Musical Times*, September 1871, p. 221
9 *ibid.*
10 *ibid.*
11 *A Short History of Cheap Music*, pp. 96–7
12 *The Musical Times*, July 1873, pp. 143–58
13 *ibid.*
14 *ibid.*
15 *ibid.*

CHAPTER EIGHT

1 Novello catalogue, 1893. Novello
2 *ibid.*
3 *ibid.*
4 Novello
5 *ibid.*
6 Novello catalogue, 1893. Novello
7 *The Musical Times*, July 1857, pp. 71–4
8 *The Musical Times*, September 1941, Supplement. Facsimile reprint. Whereabouts of original letter unknown.
9 *The Musical Times*, July 1900, p. 456
10 Private
11 *ibid.*

CHAPTER NINE

1 Private
2 *ibid.*
3 *ibid.*
4 *ibid.*
5 *A Century and a Half in Soho*, pp. 29–30
6 Royal College of Music: Sir George Grove–Edith Oldham correspondence, 4 March 1894
7 *The Musical Times*, June 1888, pp. 329–32
8 *Mirror of Music*: ed. Dr Percy Scholes. Novello/OUP, 1947, p. 254
9 Novello
10 Directors' minutes, March 1899. Novello

11 *ibid.*, October 1901
12 *ibid.*, October 1902
13 *ibid.*, January 1905 and April 1906
14 *ibid.*, April 1906
15 *The Buildings of England: London* by Nikolaus Pevsner. Penguin Books
16 *The Musical Times*, December 1906, pp. 797–802

CHAPTER TEN
1 *The Musical Times*, June 1892, p. 374
2 *Spectator*, 25 December 1909
3 Directors' minutes, October 1919. Novello
4 *ibid.*, April 1920
5 *ibid.*
6 *ibid.*, February 1927
7 *ibid.*, January 1911

CHAPTER ELEVEN
1 *The Musical Times*, November 1956, p. 578
2 *ibid.*
3 Directors' minutes, May 1928. Novello
4 *ibid.*
5 *ibid.*, March 1936
6 *ibid.*, April 1936
7 *ibid.*
8 *ibid.*, May 1921
9 *ibid.*
10 *ibid.* October 1920
11 *ibid.*
12 *The Musical Times*, February 1941, pp. 51–2

CHAPTER THIRTEEN
1 *Musical World*, i, January 1836. Front cover of wrappers
2 *ibid.*, pp. 7–8
3 *Musical World*, 10 June 1836, p. 2 of wrapper
4 *The Musical Times*, May 1875, p. 96
5 *ibid.*
6 *The Musical Times*, January 1883, p. 56
7 *ibid.*
8 *The Musical Times*, June 1892, p. 374
9 *The Musical Times*, October 1845, p. 170
10 *The Musical Times*, February 1868, pp. 292–3
11 *The Musical Times*, June 1894, pp. 369–85
12 *The Musical Times*, July 1960, p. 417

INDEX